P9-AFE-120

hooked

ALSO BY NIR EYAL

*Indistractable: How to Control Your
Attention and Choose Your Life*

hooked

HOW TO BUILD HABIT-FORMING PRODUCTS

Nir Eyal

with Ryan Hoover

BUSINESS

PENGUIN BUSINESS

UK | USA | Canada | Ireland | Australia
India | New Zealand | South Africa

Penguin Business is part of the Penguin Random House group of companies
whose addresses can be found at global.penguinrandomhouse.com.

First published in the United States of America by Portfolio/Penguin,
a member of Penguin Group (USA) LLC 2014
First published in Great Britain by Portfolio Penguin 2014
This updated edition published in Penguin Business 2019
014

Copyright © Nir Eyal, 2014, 2019

The moral right of the author has been asserted

Hooked was previously published by the author.

Printed and bound in Great Britain by Clays Ltd, Elcograf S.p.A.

A CIP catalogue record for this book is available from the British Library

ISBN: 978–0–241–18483–7

www.greenpenguin.co.uk

MIX
Paper from
responsible sources
FSC
www.fsc.org   FSC® C018179

Penguin Random House is committed to a
sustainable future for our business, our readers
and our planet. This book is made from Forest
Stewardship Council® certified paper.

| For Julie |

|contents|

| An Important Note From Nir |

Since first publishing this book, I've been blown away by the amazing stories I've heard from readers who have used these techniques to build life-changing products and services. I'm particularly impressed by the ways the book's lessons have been applied to improve not only the lives of the products' users, but the lives of the product makers as well.

Some examples: Kahoot!, a Norwegian start-up making classroom education more engaging and fun, recently filed for an initial public offering. Fitbod, an app that helps users build healthy exercise habits in the gym, is making millions of dollars for the developers. Paga, which serves millions of previously unbanked Africans, helps them form new habits of saving and managing money and is building "the single largest network of financial access points" in the country, according to the company founder. The list of companies who have used the Hooked Model continues to grow around the world in every conceivable industry.

Though many of the examples in the book draw upon big companies like Google and Facebook, I didn't write the book for them. I wrote the book for you!

The tech giants already know these techniques. My goal

is to unlock their secrets for the benefit of businesses who want to design and help users develop healthy habits.

To that end, there's so much I wanted to put in this book that just didn't fit. Before you start reading, please take a moment to download these supplementary materials, included free with the purchase of this book, at

http://www.NirAndFar.com/Hooked:

- The Hooked Model workbook
- An ebook of case studies
- A free e-mail course about product psychology

Also, if you'd like to connect with me, you can reach me through my blog at NirAndFar.com, where you can schedule office hours to discuss your questions.

I look forward to hearing from you as you build habits for good.

| introduction |

Seventy-nine percent of smartphone owners check their device within fifteen minutes of waking up every morning.[1] Perhaps more startling, fully one-third of Americans say they would rather give up sex than lose their cell phones.[2]

A 2011 university study suggested people check their phones thirty-four times per day.[3] However, industry insiders believe that number is closer to an astounding 150 daily sessions.[4]

Face it: We're hooked.

It's the pull to visit YouTube, Facebook, or Twitter for just a few minutes, only to find yourself still tapping and scrolling an hour later. It's the urge you likely feel throughout your day but hardly notice.

Cognitive psychologists define *habits* as "automatic behaviors triggered by situational cues": things we do with little or no conscious thought.[5] The products and services we use habitually alter our everyday behavior, just as their designers intended.[6] Our actions have been engineered.

How do companies, producing little more than bits of

code displayed on a screen, seemingly control users' minds? What makes some products so habit forming?

Forming habits is imperative for the survival of many products. As infinite distractions compete for our attention, companies are learning to master novel tactics to stay relevant in users' minds. Amassing millions of users is no longer good enough. Companies increasingly find that their economic value is a function of the strength of the habits they create. In order to win the loyalty of their users and create a product that's regularly used, companies must learn not only what compels users to click but also what makes them tick.

Although some companies are just waking up to this new reality, others are already cashing in. By mastering habit-forming product design, the companies profiled in this book make their goods indispensable.

FIRST TO MIND WINS

Companies that form strong user habits enjoy several benefits to their bottom line. These companies attach their product to *internal triggers*. As a result, users show up without any external prompting.

Instead of relying on expensive marketing, habit-forming companies link their services to the users' daily routines and emotions.[7] A habit is at work when users feel a tad bored and instantly open Twitter. They feel a pang of loneliness and before rational thought occurs, they are scrolling through their Facebook feeds. A question comes to mind and before searching their brains, they query Google. The first-to-mind solution wins. In chapter 1 of this book, we explore the competitive advantages of habit-forming products.

How do products create habits? The answer: The ad industry once created consumer desire during Madison Avenue's golden era, but those days are long gone. A multiscreen world of ad-wary consumers has rendered big-budget brainwashing inaccessible to all but the biggest brands.

Today, small start-up teams can profoundly change behavior by guiding users through a series of experiences I call *hooks*. The more often users run through these hooks, the more likely they are to form habits.

How I Got Hooked

In 2008 I was among a team of Stanford MBAs starting a company backed by some of the brightest investors in Silicon Valley. Our mission was to build a platform for placing advertising into the booming world of online social games.

Notable companies were making hundreds of millions of dollars selling virtual cows on digital farms while advertisers were spending huge sums of money to influence people to buy whatever they were peddling. I admit I didn't get it at first and found myself standing at the water's edge wondering, "How do they do it?"

At the intersection of these two industries dependent on mind manipulation, I embarked upon a journey to learn how products change our actions and, at times, create compulsions. How did these companies engineer user behavior? What were the moral implications of building potentially addictive products? Most important, could the same forces that made these experiences so compelling also be used to build products to improve people's lives?

Where could I find the blueprints for forming habits? To my disappointment, I found no guide. Businesses skilled in behavior design guarded their secrets, and although I uncovered books, white papers, and blog posts tangentially related to the topic, there was no how-to manual for building habit-forming products.

I began documenting my observations of hundreds of

companies to uncover patterns in user-experience designs and functionality. Although every business had its unique flavor, I sought to identify the commonalities behind the winners and understand what was missing among the losers.

I looked for insights from academia, drawing upon consumer psychology, human-computer interaction, and behavioral economics research. In 2011 I began sharing what I learned and started working as a consultant to a host of Silicon Valley companies, from small start-ups to Fortune 500 enterprises. Each client provided an opportunity to test my theories, draw new insights, and refine my thinking. I began blogging about what I learned at NirAndFar.com, and my essays were syndicated to other sites. Readers soon began writing in with their own observations and examples.

In the fall of 2012 Dr. Baba Shiv and I designed and taught a class at the Stanford Graduate School of Business on the science of influencing human behavior. The next year, I partnered with Dr. Steph Habif to teach a similar course at the Hasso Plattner Institute of Design.

These years of distilled research and real-world experience resulted in the creation of the Hooked Model: a four-phase process companies use to form habits.

Through consecutive Hook cycles, successful products reach their ultimate goal of unprompted user engagement, bringing users back repeatedly, without depending on costly advertising or aggressive messaging.

While I draw many examples from technology companies given my industry background, hooks are everywhere—
in apps, sports, movies, games, and even our jobs. Hooks
can be found in virtually any experience that burrows into
our minds (and often our wallets). The four steps of the
Hooked Model provide the framework for the chapters of
this book.

The Hooked Model

1. Trigger

A *trigger* is the actuator of behavior—the spark plug in the engine. Triggers come in two types: external and internal.[8] Habit-forming products start by alerting users with external triggers like an e-mail, a Web site link, or the app icon on a phone.

For example, suppose Barbra, a young woman in Pennsylvania, happens to see a photo in her Facebook News Feed taken by a family member from a rural part of the state. It's a lovely picture and because she is planning a trip there with her brother Johnny, the external trigger's call to action (in marketing and advertising lingo) intrigues her and she clicks. By cycling through successive hooks, users begin to form associations with internal triggers, which attach to existing behaviors and emotions.

When users start to automatically cue their next behavior, the new habit becomes part of their everyday routine. Over time, Barbra associates Facebook with her need for social connection. Chapter 2 explores external and internal triggers, answering the question of how product designers determine which triggers are most effective.

2. Action

Following the trigger comes the action: the behavior done in anticipation of a reward. The simple action of clicking on the interesting picture in her news feed takes Barbra to a

Web site called Pinterest, a "social bookmarking site with a virtual pinboard."[9]

This phase of the Hook, as described in chapter 3, draws upon the art and science of usability design to reveal how products drive specific user actions. Companies leverage two basic pulleys of human behavior to increase the likelihood of an action occurring: the ease of performing an action and the psychological motivation to do it.[10]

Once Barbra completes the simple action of clicking on the photo, she is dazzled by what she sees next.

3. Variable Reward

What distinguishes the Hooked Model from a plain vanilla feedback loop is the Hook's ability to create a craving. Feedback loops are all around us, but predictable ones don't create desire. The unsurprising response of your fridge light turning on when you open the door doesn't drive you to keep opening it again and again. However, add some variability to the mix—suppose a different treat magically appears in your fridge every time you open it—and voilà, intrigue is created.

Variable rewards are one of the most powerful tools companies implement to hook users; chapter 4 explains them in further detail. Research shows that levels of the neurotransmitter dopamine surge when the brain is expecting a reward.[11] Although dopamine is often wrongly categorized as making us feel good, introducing variability does create a focused state, which suppresses the areas of the brain associated with judgment and reason while activating the parts associated with wanting and desire.[12] Although classic examples include slot machines and lotteries, variable rewards are prevalent in many other habit-forming products.

When Barbra lands on Pinterest, not only does she see the image she intended to find, but she is also served a multitude of other glittering objects. The images are related to what she is generally interested in—namely things to see on her upcoming trip to rural Pennsylvania—but there are other things that catch her eye as well. The exciting juxtaposition of relevant and irrelevant, tantalizing and plain, beautiful and common, sets her brain's dopamine system aflutter with the promise of reward. Now she's spending more time on Pinterest, hunting for the next wonderful thing to find. Before she knows it, she's spent forty-five minutes scrolling.

Chapter 4 also explores why some people eventually lose their taste for certain experiences and how variability impacts their retention.

4. Investment

The last phase of the Hooked Model is where the user does a bit of work. The investment phase increases the odds that the user will make another pass through the cycle in the future. The investment occurs when the user puts something into the product of service such as time, data, effort, social capital, or money.

However, the investment phase isn't about users opening up their wallets and moving on with their day. Rather, the investment implies an action that improves the service for the next go-around. Inviting friends, stating preferences, building virtual assets, and learning to use new features are all investments users make to improve their experience. These commitments can be leveraged to make the trigger more engaging, the action easier, and the reward more exciting with every pass through the Hooked Model. Chapter 5 delves into how investments encourage users to cycle through successive hooks.

As Barbra enjoys scrolling through the Pinterest cornucopia, she builds a desire to keep the things that delight her. By collecting items, she gives the site data about her preferences. Soon she will follow, pin, repin, and make other investments, which serve to increase her ties to the site and prime her for future loops through Pinterest's Hook.

A New Superpower

Habit-forming technology is already here, and it is being used to shape our lives. The fact that we have greater access to the web through our various connected devices—smartphones and tablets, televisions, game consoles, and wearable technology—gives companies far greater ability to affect our behavior.

As companies combine their increased connectivity to consumers, with the ability to collect, mine, and process customer data at faster speeds, we are faced with a future where everything becomes potentially more habit forming. As famed Silicon Valley investor Paul Graham writes, "Unless the forms of technological progress that produced these things are subject to different laws than technological progress in general, the world will get more addictive in the next 40 years than it did in the last 40."[13] Chapter 6 explores this new reality and discusses the morality of manipulation.

Recently, a blog reader e-mailed me, "If it can't be used for evil, it's not a superpower." He's right. And under this definition, building habit-forming products is indeed a superpower. If used irresponsibly, bad habits can quickly degenerate into mindless, zombielike addictions for some users.

Did you recognize Barbra and her brother Johnny from the previous example? Zombie film buffs likely did. They are characters from the classic horror flick *Night of the Living Dead*, a story about people possessed by a mysterious force, which compels their every action.[14]

No doubt you've noticed the resurgence of the zombie genre over the past several years. Games like *Resident Evil*, television shows like *The Walking Dead*, and movies including *World War Z* are a testament to the creatures' growing appeal. But why are zombies suddenly so fascinating? Perhaps technology's unstoppable progress—ever more pervasive and persuasive—has grabbed us in a fearful malaise at the thought of being involuntarily controlled.

Although the fear is palpable, we are like the heroes in every zombie film—threatened but ultimately more powerful. I have come to learn that habit-forming products can do far more good than harm. Choice architecture, a concept described by famed scholars Thaler, Sunstein, and Balz in their same-titled scholarly paper, offers techniques to influence people's decisions and affect behavioral outcomes. Ultimately, though, the practice should be "used to help nudge people to make better choices (as judged by themselves)."[15] Accordingly, this book teaches innovators how to build products to help people do the things they already want to do but, for lack of a well-designed solution, don't do.

Hooked seeks to unleash the tremendous new powers innovators and entrepreneurs have to influence the everyday lives of billions of people. I believe the trinity of access, data, and speed presents unprecedented opportunities to create positive habits.

When harnessed correctly, technology can enhance lives through healthful behaviors that improve our relationships, make us smarter, and increase productivity.

The Hooked Model explains the rationale behind the design of many successful habit-forming products and services we use daily. Although not exhaustive given the vast amount of academic literature available, the model is intended to be a practical tool (rather than a theoretical one) made for entrepreneurs and innovators who aim to use habits for good. In this book I have compiled the most relevant research, shared actionable insights, and provided a practical framework designed to increase the innovator's odds of success.

Hooks connect the user's problem with a company's solution frequently enough to form a habit. My goal is to provide you with a deeper understanding of how certain products change what we do and, by extension, who we are.

HOW TO USE THIS BOOK

At the end of each section, you'll find a few bulleted takeaways. Reviewing them, jotting them down in a notebook, or sharing them on a social network is a great way to pause, reflect, and reinforce what you have read.

Building a habit-forming product yourself? If so, the "Do This Now" sections at the end of subsequent chapters will help guide your next steps.

REMEMBER & SHARE

- *Habits* are defined as "behaviors done with little or no conscious thought."

- The convergence of access, data, and speed is making the world a more habit-forming place.

- Businesses that create customer habits gain a significant competitive advantage.

- The Hooked Model describes an experience designed to connect the user's problem to a company's product frequently enough to form a habit.

- The Hooked Model has four phases: *trigger, action, variable reward,* and *investment*.

| 1 |

The Habit Zone

When I run, I zone out. I don't think about what my body is doing and my mind usually wanders elsewhere. I find it relaxing and refreshing, and run about three mornings each week. Recently, I needed to take an overseas client call during my usual morning run time. "No biggie," I thought. "I can run in the evening instead." However, the time shift created some peculiar behaviors that night.

I left the house for my run at dusk and as I was about to pass a woman taking out her trash, she made eye contact and smiled. I politely saluted her with "Good morning!" and then caught my mistake: "I mean, good evening! Sorry!" I corrected myself, realizing I was about ten hours off. She furrowed her brow and cracked a nervous smile.

Slightly embarrassed, I noted how my mind had been oblivious to the time of day. I chided myself not to do it again, but within a few minutes I passed another runner and again—as if possessed—I blurted out, "Good morning!" What was going on?

Back home, during my normal post-run shower, my mind began to wander again as it often does when I bathe.

My brain's autopilot switch turned on and I proceeded with my daily routine, unaware of my actions.

It wasn't until I felt the nick of the razor cutting my face that I realized I had lathered up and started shaving. Although it is something I do every morning, shaving was painfully unnecessary in the evening. And yet I'd done it anyway, unknowingly.

The evening version of my morning run had triggered a behavioral script that instructed my body to carry out my usual run-related activities—all without mindful awareness. Such is the nature of ingrained habits—behaviors done with little or no conscious thought—which, by some estimates, guide nearly half of our daily actions.[1]

Habits are one of the ways the brain learns complex behaviors. Neuroscientists believe habits give us the ability to focus our attention on other things by storing automatic responses in the basal ganglia, an area of the brain associated with involuntary actions.[2]

Habits form when the brain takes a shortcut and stops actively deliberating over what to do next.[3] The brain quickly learns to codify behaviors that provide a solution to whatever situation it encounters.

For example, nail biting is a common behavior that occurs with little or no conscious thought. Initially, the biter might start chomping on her fingernail for a reason—to remove an unsightly hangnail, for example. However, when the behavior occurs for no conscious purpose—simply as an automatic response to a cue—the habit is in control. For many persistent nail-biters, the unconscious trigger is the unpleasant feeling of stress. The more the biter associates the act of nail chomping with the temporary relief it provides, the harder it becomes to change the conditioned response.

Like nail biting, many of our daily decisions are made simply because that was the way we have found resolution in the past. The brain automatically deduces that if the decision was a good one yesterday, then it is a safe bet again today and the action becomes a routine.

On my run my brain had associated making eye contact with another person during my run with the standard "Good morning!" greeting; thus I automatically uttered these words no matter how inappropriately timed.

WHY HABITS ARE GOOD FOR BUSINESS

If our programmed behaviors are so influential in guiding our everyday actions, surely harnessing the same power of habits can be a boon for industry. Indeed, for those able to shape them in an effective way, habits can be very good for the bottom line.

Habit-forming products change user behavior and create unprompted user engagement. The aim is to influence customers to use your product on their own, again and again, without relying on overt calls to action such as ads or promotions. Once a habit is formed, the user is automatically triggered to use the product during routine events such as wanting to kill time while waiting in line.

However, the framework and practices explored in this book are not "one size fits all" and do not apply to every business or industry. Entrepreneurs should evaluate how user habits impact their particular business model and goals. While the viability of some products depends on habit-formation to thrive, that is not always the case.

For example, companies selling infrequently bought or used products or services do not require habitual users—at least, not in the sense of everyday engagement. Life insurance companies, for instance, leverage salespeople, advertising, and word-of-mouth referrals and recommendations to prompt consumers to buy policies. Once the policy is bought, there is nothing more the customer needs to do.

In this book I refer to products in the context of businesses that require ongoing, unprompted user engagement and therefore need to build user habits. I exclude companies that compel customers to take action through other means.

Before diving into the mechanics of how habits are made, we must first understand their general importance and competitive benefits for businesses. Habit formation is good for business in several ways.

Increasing Customer Lifetime Value

MBAs are taught that a business is worth the sum of its future profits. This benchmark is how investors calculate the fair price of a company's shares.

CEOs and their management teams are evaluated by their ability to increase the value of their stocks—and therefore care deeply about the ability of their companies to generate free cash flow. Management's job, in the eyes of shareholders, is to implement strategies to grow future profits by increasing revenues or decreasing expenses.

Fostering consumer habits is an effective way to increase the value of a company by driving higher customer lifetime value (CLTV): the amount of money made from a customer before that person switches to a competitor, stops using the product, or dies. User habits increase how long and how frequently customers use a product, resulting in higher CLTV.

Some products have a very high CLTV. For example, credit card customers tend to stay loyal for a very long time and are worth a bundle. Hence, credit card companies are willing to spend a considerable amount of money acquiring new customers. This explains why you receive so many promotional offers, ranging from free gifts to airline bonus miles, to entice you to add another card or upgrade your current one. Your potential CLTV justifies a credit card company's marketing investment.

Providing Pricing Flexibility

Renowned investor and Berkshire Hathaway CEO Warren Buffett once said, "You can determine the strength of a business over time by the amount of agony they go through in raising prices."[4] Buffett and his partner, Charlie Munger, realized that as customers form routines around a product, they come to depend upon it and become less sensitive to price. The duo have pointed to consumer psychology as the rationale behind their famed investments in companies like See's Candies and Coca-Cola.[5] Buffett and Munger understand that habits give companies greater flexibility to increase prices.

For example, in the free-to-play video game business, it is standard practice for game developers to delay asking users to pay money until they have played consistently and habitually. Once the compulsion to play is in place and the desire to progress in the game increases, converting users into paying customers is much easier. The real money lies in selling virtual items, extra lives, and special powers.

As of December 2013, more than 500 million people have downloaded *Candy Crush Saga*, a game played mostly on mobile devices. The game's "freemium" model converts some of those users into paying customers, netting the game's maker nearly $1 million per day.[6]

Supercharging Growth

Users who continuously find value in a product are more likely to tell their friends about it. Frequent usage creates more opportunities to encourage people to invite their friends, broadcast content, and share through word of mouth. Hooked users become brand evangelists—megaphones for your company, bringing in new users at little or no cost.

Products with higher user engagement also have the potential to grow faster than their rivals. Case in point: Facebook leapfrogged its competitors, including MySpace and Friendster, even though it was relatively late to the social networking party. Although its competitors both had healthy growth rates and millions of users by the time Mark Zuckerberg's fledgling site launched beyond the closed doors of academia, his company came to dominate the industry.

Facebook's success was, in part, a result of what I call the *more is more* principle—more frequent usage drives more viral growth. As David Skok, tech entrepreneur turned venture capitalist, points out, "The most important factor to increasing growth is . . . Viral Cycle Time."[7] Viral Cycle Time is the amount of time it takes a user to invite another user, and it can have a massive impact. "For example, after 20 days with a cycle time of two days, you will have 20,470 users," Skok writes. "But if you halved that cycle time to one day, you would have over 20 million users! It is logical that it would be better to have more cycles occur, but it is less obvious just how much better."

Having a greater proportion of users daily returning to a service dramatically decreases Viral Cycle Time for two reasons: First, daily users initiate loops more often (think tagging a friend in a Facebook photo); second, more daily active users means more people to respond and react to each invitation. The cycle not only perpetuates the process—with higher and higher user engagement, it accelerates it.

Sharpening the Competitive Edge

User habits are a competitive advantage. Products that change customer routines are less susceptible to attacks from other companies.

Many entrepreneurs fall into the trap of building products that are only marginally better than existing solutions, hoping their innovation will be good enough to woo customers away from existing products. But when it comes to shaking consumers' old habits, these naive entrepreneurs often find that better products don't always win—especially if a large number of users have already adopted a competing product.

A classic paper by John Gourville, a professor of marketing at Harvard Business School, stipulates that "many innovations fail because consumers irrationally overvalue the old while companies irrationally overvalue the new."[8]

Gourville claims that for new entrants to stand a chance, they can't just be better, they must be nine times better. Why such a high bar? Because old habits die hard and new products or services need to offer dramatic improvements to shake users out of old routines. Gourville writes that products that require a high degree of behavior change are doomed to fail even if the benefits of using the new product are clear and substantial.

For example, the technology I am using to write this book is inferior to existing alternatives in many ways. I'm referring to the QWERTY keyboard which was first developed in the 1870s for the now-ancient typewriter. QWERTY was designed with commonly used characters spaced far apart. This layout prevented typists from jamming the metal type bars of early machines.[9] This physical limitation is an anachronism in the digital age, yet QWERTY keyboards remain the standard despite the invention of far better layouts. Professor August Dvorak's keyboard design, for example, placed vowels in the center row, increasing typing speed and accuracy. Though patented in 1932, the Dvorak Simplified Keyboard was written off. QWERTY survives due to the high costs of changing user behavior. When first introduced to the keyboard, we use the hunt-and-peck method. After months of practice, we instinctively learn to activate all our fingers in response to our thoughts with little-to-no conscious effort, and the words begin to flow effortlessly from mind to screen. But switching to an unfamiliar keyboard—even if more efficient—would force us to relearn how to type. Fat chance!

As we will learn in chapter 5, users also increase their dependency on habit-forming products by *storing value* in them—further reducing the likelihood of switching to an alternative. For example, every e-mail sent and received using Google's Gmail is stored indefinitely, providing users with a lasting repository of past conversations. New followers on Twitter increase users' clout and amplify their ability to transmit messages to their communities. Memories and experiences captured on Instagram are added to one's digital scrapbook. Switching to a new e-mail service, social network, or photo-sharing app becomes more difficult the more people use them. The nontransferable value created and stored inside these services discourages users from leaving.

Ultimately, user habits increase a business's return on investment. Higher customer lifetime value, greater pricing flexibility, supercharged growth, and a sharpened competitive edge together equal a more powerful bang for the company's buck.

Building the Mind Monopoly

While user habits are a boon to companies fortunate enough to engender them, their existence inherently makes success less likely for new innovations and start-ups trying to disrupt the status quo. The fact is that successfully changing long-term user habits is exceptionally rare.

Altering behavior requires not only an understanding of how to persuade people to act—for example, the first time they land on a web page—but also necessitates getting them to repeat behaviors for long periods, ideally for the rest of their lives.

Companies that succeed in building a habit-forming business are often associated with game-changing, wildly successful innovation. But like any discipline, habit design has rules and caveats that define and explain why some products change lives while others do not.

For one, new behaviors have a short half-life, as our minds tend to revert to our old ways of thinking and doing. Experiments show that lab animals habituated to new behaviors tend to regress to their first learned behaviors over time.[10] To borrow a term from accounting, behaviors are LIFO—"last in, first out." In other words, the habits you've most recently acquired are also the ones most likely to go soonest.

This helps explain the overwhelming evidence that people rarely change their habits for long. Two-thirds of alcoholics who complete a rehabilitation program will pick up the bottle, and their old habits, within a year's time.[11] Research shows that nearly everyone who loses weight on a diet gains back the pounds within two years.[12]

The enemy of forming new habits is past behaviors, and research suggests that old habits die hard. Even when we change our routines, neural pathways remain etched in our brains, ready to be reactivated when we lose focus.[13] This presents an especially difficult challenge for product designers trying to create new lines or businesses based on forming new habits.

For new behaviors to really take hold, they must occur often. In a recent study at the University College London, researchers followed participants as they attempted to form a habit of flossing their teeth.[14] As one of its findings, the study concluded that the more frequently the new behavior occurred, the stronger the habit became. Like flossing, frequent engagement with a product—especially over a short period of time—increases the likelihood of forming new routines.

Google Search provides an example of a service built upon a frequent behavior that helped create users' habits. If you're skeptical that Google is habit forming (and you are a frequent Google user), just try using Bing. In a head-to-head comparison of the efficacy of an incognito search, the products are nearly identical.[15] Even if the geniuses at Google have in fact perfected a faster algorithm, the time saved is imperceptible.

So why haven't more Google users switched to Bing? Habits keep users loyal. If a user is familiar with the Google interface, switching to Bing requires cognitive effort. Although many aspects of Bing are similar to Google, even a slight change in pixel placement forces the would-be user to learn a new way of interacting with the site. Adapting to the differences in the Bing interface is what actually slows down regular Google users and makes Bing feel inferior, not the technology itself.

Internet searches occur so frequently that Google is able to cement itself as the one and only solution in the habituated user's mind. Users no longer need to think about whether or not to use Google; they just do. Furthermore, whenever the company can identify the user through tracking technology, it improves search results based on past behaviors to deliver a more accurate and personalized experience, reinforcing the user's connection with the search engine. The more the product is used, the better the algorithm gets, and thus the more it is used. The result is a virtuous cycle of habit-driven behavior resulting in Google's market domination.[16]

HABIT AS STRATEGY

Sometimes a behavior does not occur as frequently as flossing or Googling, but it still becomes a habit. For an infrequent action to become a habit, the user must perceive a high degree of utility, either from gaining pleasure or avoiding pain.

Take Amazon as an example: The e-tailer has its sights set on becoming the world's one-stop shop. Amazon is so confident in its ability to form user habits that it sells and runs ads for directly competitive products on its site.[17] Customers often see the item they are about to buy listed at a cheaper price and can click away to transact elsewhere. To some, this sounds like a formula for disaster. But to Amazon, it is a shrewd business strategy.

Not only does Amazon make money from the ads it runs from competing businesses, it also utilizes other companies' marketing dollars to form a habit in the shopper's mind. Amazon seeks to become the solution to a frequently occurring pain point—the customer's desire to find the items they want.

By addressing shoppers' price concerns, Amazon earns loyalty even if it doesn't make the sale and comes across as trustworthy in the process. The tactic is backed by a 2003 study, which demonstrated that consumers' preference for an online retailer increases when they are offered competitive price information.[18] The technique has also been used by Progressive, the car insurance company, to drive over $15 billion of annual insurance sales, up from just $3.4 billion before the tactic was implemented.

By allowing users to comparison shop from within the site, Amazon provides tremendous perceived utility to its customers. Although shopping on Amazon may not occur as frequently as searching on Google, the company solidifies its place as the default solution to customers' purchasing needs with each successful transaction. In fact, people are so comfortable comparison shopping on Amazon that they frequently use the company's mobile app to check prices when standing in the aisles of real stores—often making a purchase from inside a competing retailer.[19]

In the Habit Zone

A company can begin to determine its product's habit-forming potential by plotting two factors: *frequency* (how often the behavior occurs) and *perceived utility* (how useful and rewarding the behavior is in the user's mind over alternative solutions).

Googling occurs multiple times per day, but any particular search is negligibly better than rival services like Bing. Conversely, using Amazon may be a less frequent occurrence,

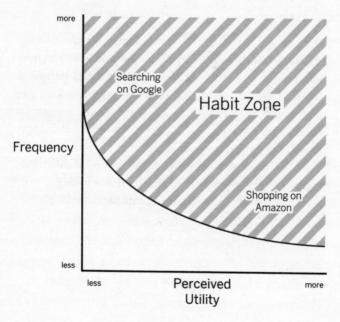

FIGURE 1

but users receive great value knowing they'll find whatever they need at the one and only "everything store."[20]

As represented in figure 1, a behavior that occurs with enough frequency and perceived utility enters the *Habit Zone*, helping to make it a default behavior. If either of these factors falls short and the behavior lies below the threshold, it is less likely that the desired behavior will become a habit.

Note that the line slopes downward but never quite reaches the perceived utility axis. Some behaviors never become habits because they do not occur frequently enough. No matter how much utility is involved, infrequent behaviors remain conscious actions and never create the automatic response that is characteristic of habits. On the other axis, however, even a behavior that provides minimal perceived benefit can become a habit simply because it occurs frequently.

Remember, the Hooked Model does not get people to do things they don't want to do. Your product must ultimately be useful. The *Habit Zone* is meant to be a guiding theory, and the scale of the illustration is intentionally left blank. Unfortunately for companies, research thus far has not found a universal timescale for turning all behaviors into habits. A 2010 study found that some habits can be formed in a matter of weeks while others can take more than five months.[21] The researchers also found that the complexity of the behavior and how important the habit was to the person greatly affected how quickly the routine was formed.

There are few rules when it comes to answering "How

frequent is frequent enough?" and the answer is likely specific to each business and behavior. However, as the previously mentioned flossing study demonstrates, we know that
higher frequency is better.

Think of the products and services you would identify
as habit forming. Most of these are used daily, if not multiple times per day. Let's explore why we use these products
so frequently.

Vitamins Versus Painkillers

It's never been easier to launch a new product or service,
yet most new endeavors fail. Why? Products fail for a variety
of reasons: Companies run out of funding, products enter
markets too early or too late, the marketplace doesn't need
what companies are offering, or founders simply give up.
Just as failure has many causes, success too can be attributed
to a variety of factors. However, one aspect is common to all
successful innovations—they solve problems. That may seem
obvious, but understanding the kind of problem a new
product solves can be a topic of much debate.

"Are you building a vitamin or painkiller?" is a common,
almost clichéd question many investors ask founders eager to
cash their first venture capital check. The correct answer, from
the perspective of most investors, is the latter: a painkiller.
Likewise, innovators in companies big and small are constantly asked to prove their idea is important enough to merit

the time and money needed to build it. Gatekeepers such as investors and managers want to invest in solving real problems or meeting immediate needs by backing painkillers.

Painkillers solve an obvious need, relieving a specific pain, and often have quantifiable markets.

Think Tylenol, the brand-name version of acetaminophen, and the product's promise of reliable relief. It's the kind of ready-made solution for which people are happy to pay.

Vitamins, by contrast, do not necessarily solve an obvious pain point. Instead they appeal to users' emotional rather than functional needs.

When we take our multivitamin each morning, we don't really know if it is actually making us healthier. In fact, recent evidence shows taking multivitamins may actually be doing more harm than good.[22]

But we don't really care, do we? Efficacy is not why we take vitamins. Taking a vitamin is a "check it off your list" behavior we measure in terms of psychological, rather than physical, relief. We feel satisfied that we are doing something good for our bodies—even if we can't tell how much good it is actually doing us.

Unlike a painkiller, without which we cannot function, missing a few days of vitamin popping, say while on vacation, is no big deal. So perhaps managers and investors know best? Perhaps building painkillers, not vitamins, is always the right strategy.

Not so fast.

Let's consider a few of today's hottest consumer technology companies: Facebook, Twitter, Instagram, and Pinterest. What are they selling—vitamins or painkillers? Most people would guess vitamins, thinking users aren't doing much of anything important other than perhaps seeking a quick boost of social validation. After all, think back to before you first started using these services. No one ever woke up in the middle of the night screaming, "I need something to help me update my status!"

But like so many innovations, we did not know we needed them until they became part of our everyday lives. Before making up your mind on the vitamin versus painkiller debate for some of the world's most successful tech companies, consider this idea: A habit is when not doing an action causes a bit of discomfort.

The sensation is similar to an *itch*, a feeling that manifests within the mind until it is satisfied. The habit-forming products we use are simply there to provide some sort of relief. Using a technology or product to scratch the itch provides faster satisfaction than ignoring it. Once we come to depend on a tool, switching to something else takes work.

My answer to the vitamin versus painkiller question: Habit-forming technologies are both. These services seem at first to be offering nice-to-have vitamins, but once the habit is established, they provide an ongoing pain remedy.

Avoiding pain is a key motivator in all species. When we feel discomfort, we seek to escape the uncomfortable sensation. In the next chapter, we will explore how negative sensations trigger users to reach for solutions. For now, the important thing to remember is that habit-forming products create associations in users' minds—and that the solution to their pain may be found in your product's use.

We'll discuss the morality of manipulation in chapter 8; however, it is worth noting that although some people use the terms interchangeably, *habits* are not the same things as *addictions*. The latter describes persistent, compulsive dependencies on a behavior or substance that harms the user. Addictions, by definition, are self-destructive. Thus, it is irresponsible to make products that rely on creating and maintaining user addictions because doing so would mean intentionally hurting people.

A habit, on the other hand, is a behavior that can have a positive influence on a person's life. Habits can be healthy or unhealthy, and you likely have several helpful habits you carry out throughout your day. Did you brush your teeth today? Take a shower? Did you express gratitude by saying "Thanks"? Or in my case, use the greeting "Good morning" while on an *evening* jog? These are common behaviors done with little or no deliberation—they are habits.

Similarly, there are many opportunities to help people develop new healthy habits. Imagine if you could keep people engaged with your product or services as fervently and loyally as people check their favorite smartphone apps.

What if people learned to work out more, be more productive at work, or stayed in touch with loved ones in life-enhancing ways thanks to your product's ability to keep them coming back on their own, without the need for expensive advertising or spammy messages?

I didn't write *Hooked* for the social media companies and video game makers—they already know these tactics. I wrote this book for you, so everyone can build products that help people do what they really want, but for lack of good product design, don't.

Diving into the Hooked Model

Ready to learn more about creating positive user habits? Read on to gain a deeper understanding of the Hooked Model, a simple yet powerful way to help your customers form habits that connect their problem with your solution.

In the next chapters we dive into each phase of the Hooked Model. Along the way I will provide examples you can use in the design of your own product or service. By learning a few fundamentals of how the mind works, you will increase your odds of building the right product faster and ultimately improve the lives of your users.

REMEMBER & SHARE

- For some businesses, forming habits is a critical component to success, but not every business requires habitual user engagement.

- When successful, forming strong user habits can have several business benefits including: higher customer lifetime value (CLTV), greater pricing flexibility, supercharged growth, and a sharper competitive edge.

- Habits cannot form outside the Habit Zone, where the behavior occurs with enough frequency and perceived utility.

- Habit-forming products often start as nice-to-haves (vitamins) but once the habit is formed, they become must-haves (painkillers).

- Habit-forming products alleviate users' discomfort by relieving a pronounced itch.

- Designing habit-forming products is a form of manipulation. Product builders would benefit from a bit of introspection before attempting to hook users to make sure they are building healthy habits, not unhealthy addictions (more to come on this topic in chapter 8).

DO THIS NOW

If you are building a habit-forming product, write down the answers to these questions:

- What habits does your business model require?

- What problem are users turning to your product to solve?

- How do users currently solve that problem and why does it need a solution?

- How frequently do you expect users to engage with your product once they are habituated?

- What user behavior do you want to make into a habit?

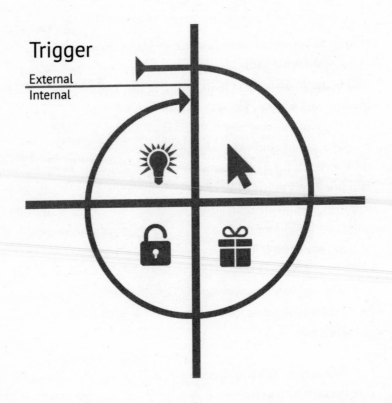

| 2 |

Trigger

Yin (not her real name) is in her mid-twenties, lives in Palo Alto, California, and attends Stanford University. She has all the composure and polish you'd expect of a student at a prestigious school, yet she succumbs to a persistent habit throughout her day. She is hooked on Instagram.

The photo- and video-sharing social network, purchased by Facebook for $1 billion in 2012, captured the minds and attention of Yin and 150 million other users like her at the time of the acquisition.[1] But by 2018, the service boasted over one billion monthly active users and was reported to be worth over $100 billion if it were a standalone entity.[2]

The company demonstrates the increasing power of—and immense monetary value created by—habit-forming technology.

Instagram is an example of an enterprising team—conversant in psychology as much as technology—that unleashed a habit-forming product on users who subsequently made it a part of their daily routines.[3]

Yin admits she regularly snaps and posts dozens of pictures per day using the app. "It's just fun," she says as she reviews her latest collection of moody snapshots filtered to look like they were taken in the late 1970s. *I just use it whenever I see something cool. I feel I need to grab it before it's gone.*

What formed Yin's Instagram habit? How did this seemingly simple app become such an important part of her life? As we will soon learn, habits like Yin's are formed over time, but the chain reaction that forms a habit always starts with a trigger.

HABITS ARE NOT CREATED, THEY ARE BUILT UPON

Habits are like pearls. Oysters create natural pearls by accumulating layer upon layer of a nacre called mother-of-pearl, eventually forming the smooth treasure over several years. But what causes the nacre to begin forming a pearl? The arrival of a tiny irritant, such as a piece of grit or an unwelcome parasite, triggers the oyster's system to begin blanketing the invader with layers of shimmery coating.

Similarly, new habits need a foundation upon which to build. Triggers provide the basis for sustained behavior change.

Reflect on your own life for a moment. What woke you up this morning? What caused you to brush your teeth? What brought you to read this book?

Triggers take the form of obvious cues like the morning alarm clock but also come as more subtle, sometimes subconscious signals that just as effectively influence our daily behavior. A trigger is the actuator of behavior—the grit in the oyster that precipitates the pearl. Whether we are cognizant of them or not, triggers move us to take action.

Triggers come in two types: *external* and *internal*.

External Triggers

Habit-forming technologies start changing behavior by first cueing users with a call to action. This sensory stimuli is delivered through any number of things in our environment.

External triggers are embedded with information, which tells the user what to do next.

An external trigger communicates the next action the user should take. Often, the desired action is made explicitly clear. For example, what external triggers do you see in this Coca-Cola vending machine in figure 2?

Take a close look at the welcoming man in the image.

FIGURE 2

He is offering you a refreshing Coke. The "Thirsty?" text below the image tells you what the man in the photo is asking and prompts the next expected action of inserting money and selecting a beverage.

Online, an external trigger may take the form of a prominent button, such as the large "Log in to Mint" prompt in the e-mail from Mint.com in figure 3. Here again, the user is given explicit instructions about what action to take after reading the e-mail: Click on that big button.

Notice how prominent and clear the intended action is in the e-mail from Mint? The company could have included several other triggers such as prompts to check your bank

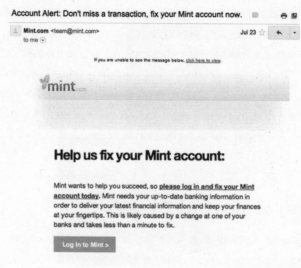

FIGURE 3

balance, view credit card deals, or set financial goals. Instead, because this is an important account alert e-mail,
Mint has reduced the available actions to a single click: logging in to view and fix your account.

More choices require the user to evaluate multiple options. Too many choices or irrelevant options can cause
hesitation, confusion, or worse—abandonment.[4] Reducing
the thinking required to take the next action increases the
likelihood of the desired behavior occurring with little
thought. We'll explore this further in the next chapter.

The Coca-Cola vending machine and Mint.com e-mail
provide good examples of explicit external triggers. However,

external triggers can also convey implicit information about the next desired user action. For example, we've all learned that Web site links are for clicking and app icons are for tapping. The only purpose for these common visual triggers is to prompt the user to action. As a readily accepted aspect of interface design, these calls to action don't need to tell people how to use them; the information is embedded.

Types of External Triggers

Companies can utilize four types of external triggers to move users to complete desired actions:

1. Paid Triggers

Advertising, search engine marketing, and other paid channels are commonly used to get users' attention and prompt them to act. Paid triggers can be effective but costly ways to keep users coming back. Habit-forming companies tend not to rely on paid triggers for very long, if at all. Imagine if YouTube, Slack, or Instagram needed to buy an ad to prompt users to revisit their sites—these companies would soon go broke.

Because paying for reengagement is unsustainable for most business models, companies generally use paid triggers to acquire new users and then leverage other triggers to bring them back.

2. Earned Triggers

Earned triggers are free in that they cannot be bought directly, but they often require investment in the form of time spent on public and media relations. Favorable press mentions, hot viral videos, and featured app store placements are all effective ways to gain attention. Companies may be lulled into thinking that related downloads or sales spikes signal long-term success, yet awareness generated by earned triggers can be short-lived.

For earned triggers to drive ongoing user acquisition, companies must keep their products in the limelight—a difficult and unpredictable task.

3. Relationship Triggers

One person telling others about a product or service can be a highly effective external trigger for action. Whether through an electronic invitation, a Facebook "like," or old fashioned word of mouth, product referrals from friends and family are often a key component of technology diffusion.

Relationship triggers can create the viral hyper-growth entrepreneurs and investors lust after. Sometimes relationship triggers drive growth because people love to tell one another about a wonderful offer.

For example, it is hard to top PayPal's viral success of the late 1990s.[5] PayPal knew that once account holders started sending other users money online they would realize the tremendous value of the service. The allure that someone just sent you money was a huge incentive to open an account, and PayPal's growth spread because it was both viral and useful.

Unfortunately, some companies utilize viral loops and relationship triggers in unethical ways: by deploying so-called dark patterns. When designers intentionally trick users into inviting friends or blasting a message to their social networks, they may see some initial growth, but it comes at the expense of users' goodwill and trust. When people discover they've been duped, they vent their frustration and stop using the product.

Proper use of relationship triggers requires building an engaged user base that is enthusiastic about sharing the benefits of the product with others.

4. Owned Triggers

Owned triggers consume a piece of real estate in the user's environment. They consistently show up in daily life and it is ultimately up to the user to opt in to allowing these triggers to appear.

For example, an app icon on the user's phone screen, an e-mail newsletter to which the user subscribes, or an app update notification only appears if the user wants it there.

As long as the user agrees to see the trigger, the company that sets the trigger *owns* a share of the user's attention.

Owned triggers are only set after users sign up for an account, submit their e-mail address, install an app, opt in to newsletters, or otherwise indicate they want to continue receiving communications.

While paid, earned, and relationship triggers drive new user acquisition, owned triggers prompt repeat engagement until a habit is formed. Without owned triggers and users' tacit permission to enter their attentional space, it is difficult to cue users frequently enough to change their behavior.

Yet external triggers are only the first step. The ultimate goal of all external triggers is to propel users into and through the Hooked Model so that, after successive cycles, they do not need further prompting from external triggers. When users form habits, they are cued by a different kind of trigger: internal ones.

Internal Triggers

When a product becomes tightly coupled with a thought, an emotion, or a preexisting routine, it leverages an internal trigger. Unlike external triggers, which use sensory stimuli like a morning alarm clock or giant "Login Now" button, you can't see, touch, or hear an internal trigger.

> *Internal triggers manifest automatically in your mind. Connecting internal triggers with a product is the brass ring of habit-forming technology.*

For Yin, the young woman with the Instagram habit, her favorite photo app manufactured a predictable response cued by an internal trigger. Through repeated conditioning, a connection was formed between Yin's need to capture images of the things around her and the app on her ever-present mobile device.

Emotions, particularly negative ones, are powerful internal triggers and greatly influence our daily routines. Feelings of boredom, loneliness, frustration, confusion, and indecisiveness often instigate a slight pain or irritation and prompt an almost instantaneous and often mindless action to quell the negative sensation. For instance, Yin often uses Instagram when she fears a special moment will be lost forever.

The severity of the discomfort may be relatively minor—perhaps her fear is below the perceptibility of consciousness—but that's exactly the point. Our life is filled with tiny stressors and we're usually unaware of our habitual reactions to these nagging issues.

Positive emotions can also serve as internal triggers, and may even be triggered themselves by a need to satisfy something that is bothering us. After all, we use products to find solutions to problems. The desire to be entertained can be thought of as the need to satiate boredom. A need to share good news can also be thought of as an attempt to find and maintain social connections.

As product designers it is our goal to solve these problems and eliminate pain—to scratch the user's itch. Users who find a product that alleviates their pain will form strong, positive associations with the product over time. After continued use, bonds begin to form—like the layers of nacre in an oyster—between the product and the user whose need it satisfies.

Gradually, these bonds cement into a habit as users turn to your product when experiencing certain internal triggers.

A study at the Missouri University of Science and Technology illustrates how tech solutions can provide frequent psychological relief.[6] In 2011 a group of 216 undergraduates volunteered to have their Internet activity anonymously tracked. Over the course of the academic year, the researchers measured the frequency with which these students used the web and what they were doing online.

At the end of the study, the researchers compared anonymous data of students who visited the university's health services to treat symptoms of depression. "We identified several features of Internet usage that correlated with depression," wrote Sriram Chellappan, one of the study's authors.[7] "For example, participants with depressive symptoms tended to engage in very high e-mail usage . . . Other characteristic features of depressive Internet behavior included increased amounts of video watching, gaming, and chatting."

The study demonstrated that people suffering from symptoms of depression used the Internet more. Why is that? One hypothesis is that those with depression experience negative emotions more frequently than the general population and seek relief by turning to technology to lift their mood.

Consider, perhaps, your own emotion-cued behaviors. What do you do in response to your internal triggers?

When bored, many people seek excitement and turn to dramatic news headlines. When we feel overly stressed, we seek serenity, perhaps finding relief with a meditation app like Headspace. When we feel lonely, we might use a social network to provide connection.

To ameliorate the sensation of uncertainty, Google is just a click away. E-mail, perhaps the mother of all habit-forming technology, is a go-to solution for many of our daily agitations, from validating our importance (or even our existence) by checking to see if someone needs us, to providing an escape from life's more mundane moments.

Once we're hooked, using these products does not always require an explicit call to action. Instead, they rely upon our automatic responses to feelings that precipitate the desired behavior. Products that attach to these internal triggers provide users with quick relief. Once a technology has created an association in users' minds that the product is the solution of choice, they return on their own, no longer needing prompts from external triggers.

> *In the case of internal triggers, the information about what to do next is encoded as a learned association in the user's memory.*

The association between an internal trigger and your product, however, is not formed overnight. It can take weeks or months of frequent usage for internal triggers to latch onto cues. New habits are sparked by external triggers, but associations with internal triggers are what keeps users hooked.

As Yin said, "I just use it whenever I see something cool." By thoughtfully moving users from external to internal triggers, Instagram designed a persistent routine in people's lives. A need is triggered in Yin's mind every time a moment is worth holding on to, and for her, the immediate solution is Instagram. Yin no longer requires an external stimulus to prompt her to use the app—the internal trigger happens on its own.

Building for Triggers

Products that successfully create habits soothe the user's pain by laying claim to a particular feeling. To do so, product designers must know their user's internal triggers—that is, the pain they seek to solve. Finding customers' internal triggers requires learning more about people than what they can tell you in a survey, though. It requires digging deeper to understand how your users feel.

> *The ultimate goal of a habit-forming product is to solve the user's pain by creating an association so that the user identifies the company's product or service as the source of relief.*

First, the company must identify the particular frustration or pain point in emotional terms, rather than product features. How do you, as a designer, go about uncovering the source of a user's pain? The best place to start is to learn the drivers behind successful habit-forming products—not to copy them, but to understand how they solve users' problems. Doing so will give you practice in diving deeper into the mind of the consumer and alert you to common human needs and desires.

As Evan Williams, cofounder of Blogger and Twitter said, the Internet is "a giant machine designed to give people what they want."[8] Williams continued, "We often think the Internet enables you to do new things . . . But people just want to do the same things they've always done."

These common needs are timeless and universal. Yet talking to users to reveal these wants will likely prove ineffective because they themselves don't know which emotions motivate them. People just don't think in these terms. You'll often find that people's *declared preferences*—what they say they want—are far different from their *revealed preferences*—what they actually do.

As Erika Hall, author of *Just Enough Research* writes, "When the research focuses on what people *actually do* (watch cat videos) rather than what they *wish they did* (produce cinema-quality home movies) it actually expands possibilities."[9] Looking for discrepancies exposes opportunities. Why do people really send text messages? Why do they take photos? What role does watching television or sports play in their lives? Ask yourself what pain these habits solve and what the user might be feeling right before one of these actions.

What would your users want to achieve by using your solution? Where and when will they use it? What emotions influence their use and will trigger them to action?

Jack Dorsey, cofounder of Twitter and Square, shared how his companies answer these important questions: "[If] you want to build a product that is relevant to folks, you need to put yourself in their shoes and you need to write a story from their side. So, we spend a lot of time writing what's called user narratives."[10]

Dorsey goes on to describe how he tries to truly understand his user: "He is in the middle of Chicago and they go to a coffee store . . . This is the experience they're going to have. It reads like a play. It's really, really beautiful. If you do that story well, then all of the prioritization, all of the product, all of the design and all the coordination that you need to do with these products just falls out naturally because you can edit the story and everyone can relate to the story from all levels of the organization, engineers to operations to support to designers to the business side of the house."

Dorsey believes a clear description of users—their desires, emotions, the context with which they use the product—is paramount to building the right solution. In addition to Dorsey's user narratives, tools like customer development,[11] usability studies, and empathy maps[12] are examples of methods for learning about potential users.

One method is to try asking the question "Why?" as many times as it takes to get to an emotion. Usually, this will happen by the fifth why. This is a technique adapted from the Toyota Production System, described by Taiichi Ohno as the "5 Whys Method." Ohno wrote that it was "the basis of Toyota's scientific approach . . . by repeating 'why?' five times, the nature of the problem as well as its solution becomes clear."[13]

When it comes to figuring out why people use habit-forming products, internal triggers are the root cause, and "Why?" is a question that can help drill right to the core.

For example, let's say we're building a fancy new technology called e-mail for the first time. The target user is a busy middle manager named Julie. We've built a detailed narrative of our user, Julie, that helps us answer the following series of whys:

Why #1: Why would Julie want to use e-mail?
Answer: So she can send and receive messages.
Why #2: Why would she want to do that?

Answer: Because she wants to share and receive
           information quickly.

Why #3: Why does she want to do that?

Answer: To know what's going on in the lives of her
           coworkers, friends, and family.

Why #4: Why does she need to know that?

Answer: To know if someone needs her.

Why #5: Why would she care about that?

Answer: She fears being out of the loop.

Now we've got something! Fear is a powerful internal trigger and we can design our solution to help calm Julie's fear. Naturally, we might have come to another conclusion by starting with a different persona, varying the narrative, or coming up with different hypothetical answers along the chain of whys. Only an accurate understanding of our user's underlying needs can inform the product requirements.

Now that we have an understanding of the user's pain, we can move on to the next step of testing our product to see if it solves his problem.

Unpacking Instagram's Triggers

A large component of Instagram's success—and what brings its millions of users back nearly every day—is the company's ability to understand its users' triggers. For people like Yin, Instagram is a harbor for emotions and inspirations, a virtual memoir preserved in pixels.

Yin's habitual use of the service started with an external trigger—a recommendation from a friend and weeks of repetitious use before she became a regular user.

Every time Yin snaps a picture, she shares it with her friends on Facebook. Consider the first time you saw an Instagram photo. Did it catch your attention? Did it make you curious? Did it call you to action?

These photos serve as a *relationship external trigger*, raising awareness and serving as a cue for others to install and use the app. But Instagram photos shared on Facebook and Twitter were not the only external triggers driving new users. Others learned of the app from the media and bloggers, or through the featured placement Apple granted Instagram in its App Store—all *earned external triggers*.

Once installed, Instagram benefited from *owned external* triggers. The app icon on users' phone screens and push notifications about their friends' postings served to call them back.

With repeated use, Instagram formed strong associations with internal triggers, and what was once a brief behavior became an intraday routine for many users.

It is the fear of losing a special moment that instigates a pang of stress. This negative emotion is the internal trigger that brings Instagram users back to the app to alleviate this pain by capturing a photo.

Yet, as users continue to use the service, new internal triggers form. Instagram is more than a camera replacement; it is a social network. The app helps users dispel boredom by connecting them with others, sharing photos, and swapping lighthearted banter.[14]

Like many social networking sites, Instagram also alleviates the increasingly recognizable pain point known as *fear of missing out,* or FOMO. For Instagram, associations with internal triggers provide a foundation to form new habits.

It is now time to understand the mechanics of connecting the user's problem with your solution by utilizing the next step in the Hooked Model. In the next chapter we'll find out how moving people from triggers to actions is critical in establishing new routines.

REMEMBER & SHARE

- *Triggers* cue the user to take action and are the first step in the Hooked Model.

- Triggers come in two types—external and internal.

- *External triggers* tell the user what to do next by placing information within the user's environment.

- *Internal triggers* tell the user what to do next through associations stored in the user's memory.

- Negative emotions frequently serve as internal triggers.

- To build a habit-forming product, makers need to attach the use of their solution to a frequently felt internal trigger and know how to leverage external triggers to drive the user to action.

DO THIS NOW

Refer to the answers you came up with in the last "Do This Now" section to complete the following exercises:

- Who is your product's user?

- What is the user doing right before your intended habit?

- Come up with three internal triggers that could cue your user to action. Refer to the 5 Whys Method described in this chapter.

- Which internal trigger does your user experience most frequently?

- Finish this brief narrative using the most frequent internal trigger and the habit you are designing: "Every time the user (internal trigger), he/she (first action of intended habit)."

- Refer back to the question about what the user is doing right before the first action of the habit. What might be places and times to send an external trigger?

- How can you couple an external trigger as closely as possible to when the user's internal trigger fires?

- Think of at least three conventional ways to trigger your user with current technology (e-mails, notifications, text messages, etc.). Then stretch yourself to come up with at least three crazy or currently impossible ideas for ways to trigger your user (wearable computers, biometric sensors, carrier pigeons, etc.). You could find that your crazy ideas spur some new approaches that may not be so nutty after all. In a few years new technologies will create all sorts of currently unimaginable triggering opportunities.

Action

| 3 |

Action

The next step in the Hooked Model is the *action phase*. The trigger, driven by internal or external cues, informs the user of what to do next; however, if the user does not take action, the trigger is useless. To initiate action, doing must be easier than thinking. Remember, a habit is a behavior done with little or no conscious thought. The more effort—either physical or mental—required to perform the desired action, the less likely it is to occur.

Action Versus Inaction

If action is paramount to habit formation, how can a product designer influence users to act? Is there a formula for behavior? It turns out that there is.

While there are many theories about what drives human behaviors, Dr. B. J. Fogg, Director of the Persuasive Technology Lab at Stanford University, has developed a model that serves as an elegant way to understand what drives our actions.

Fogg posits that there are three ingredients required to ini-
tiate any and all behaviors: (1) the user must have suffi-
cient motivation; (2) the user must have the ability to
complete the desired action; and (3) a trigger must be
present to activate the behavior.

The Fogg Behavior Model is represented in the formula
B = MAT, which represents that a given behavior will occur
when motivation, ability, and a trigger are present at the
same time and in sufficient degrees.[1] If any component of
this formula is missing or inadequate, the user will not cross
the "Action Line" and the behavior will not occur.

Let's walk through an example Fogg uses to explain his
model. Imagine a time when your mobile phone rang but
you didn't answer it. Why not?

Perhaps the phone was buried in a bag and therefore
difficult to reach. In this case your inability to easily answer
the call inhibited the action. Your ability was limited.

Maybe you thought the caller was a telemarketer or
someone else you did not want to speak to. Your lack of motivation influenced you to ignore the call.

It is possible that the call was important and within
arm's reach, but the ringer on your phone was silenced.
Despite having both a strong motivation and easy access to
answer the call, it was completely missed because you never
heard it ring—in other words, no trigger was present.

In the previous chapter we covered triggers. Let us now

dive deeper into the other two components of the Fogg Behavior Model: *motivation* and *ability*.

Motivation

While a trigger cues an action, motivation defines the level of desire to take that action. Dr. Edward Deci, Professor of Psychology at the University of Rochester and a leading researcher on the self-determination theory, defines *motivation* as "the energy for action."[2]

The nature of motivation is a widely contested topic in psychology, but Fogg argues that three Core Motivators drive our desire to act.

Fogg states that all humans are motivated to seek pleasure and avoid pain; to seek hope and avoid fear; and finally, to seek social acceptance and avoid rejection. The two sides of the three Core Motivators can be thought of as levers to increase or decrease the likelihood of someone's taking a particular action by increasing or decreasing that person's motivation.

Motivation Examples in Advertising

Perhaps no industry makes the elements of motivation more explicit than the advertising business. Advertisers regularly tap into people's motivations to influence their habits. By looking at ads with a critical eye, we can identify how they attempt to influence our actions.

For example, Barack Obama's 2008 presidential campaign leveraged a deeply inspiring message and image during a time of economic and political upheaval. An iconic poster designed by artist Shepard Fairey conveyed the idea of hope—not only printing the word in bold letters along the bottom of the image, but also through Obama's steadfast gaze as he looked confidently toward the future. (Unfortunately, because this image is at the center of a copyright battle between Fairey and the Associated Press, which claims ownership of the original photograph used in the artwork, I've chosen to not to include it here. If you can't recall the image, there is a link in the endnotes).[3]

Another example of motivation in advertising relates to the old saying "Sex sells." Long an advertising standard, images of buff, scantily clad (and usually female) bodies are used to hawk everything from the latest Victoria's Secret lingerie to domain names through GoDaddy .com and fast food chains such as Carl's Jr. and Burger King (figure 4). These and countless other ads use the voyeuristic promise of pleasure to capture attention and motivate action.

Naturally, this strategy only appeals to a particular demographic's association with sex as a salient motivator. While teenage boys—the common target for such ads— may find them inspiring, others may find them distasteful. What motivates some people will not motivate others, a fact

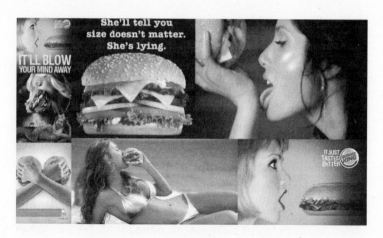

FIGURE 4

that provides all the more reason to understand the needs of your particular target audience.

Sometimes the psychological motivator is not as obvious as those used by Obama supporters or fast food chains. The Budweiser ad in figure 5 illustrates how the beer company

FIGURE 5

uses the motivator of social cohesion by displaying three pals ("buds") cheering for their national team. Although beer is not directly related to social acceptance, the ad reinforces the association that the brand goes together with good friends and good times.

On the flip side, negative emotions such as fear can also be powerful motivators. The ad in figure 6 shows a disabled man with a shocking head scar. The ad strongly communicates the risks of not wearing a motorcycle helmet. The tagline, *I won't wear a helmet it makes me look stupid*, along with the patient's post-motorcycle accident mental age (two years old), send a chilling message.

As described in the previous chapter on triggers, understanding why the user needs your product or service is critical.

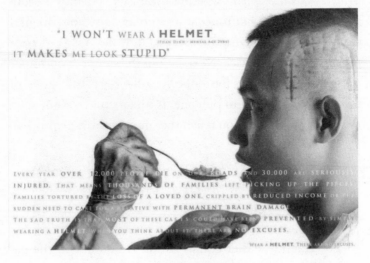

FIGURE 6

While internal triggers are the frequent, everyday itch experienced by users, the right motivators create action by offering the promise of desirable outcomes (i.e., a satisfying scratch).

However, even with the right trigger enabled and motivation running high, product designers often find users still don't behave the way they want them to. What's missing in this equation? Usability—or rather, the ability of the user to take action easily.

Ability

In his book *Something Really New: Three Simple Steps to Creating Truly Innovative Products*,[4] author Denis J. Hauptly deconstructs the process of innovation into its most fundamental steps. First, Hauptly states, understand the reason people use a product or service. Next, lay out the steps the customer must take to get the job done. Finally, once the series of tasks from intention to outcome is understood, simply start removing steps until you reach the simplest possible process.

Consequently, any technology or product that significantly reduces the steps to complete a task will enjoy high adoption rates by the people it assists.

For Hauptly, easier equals better. However, can the nature of innovation be explained so succinctly? Perhaps a brief detour into the technology of the recent past will illustrate the point.

Just twenty-five years ago a dial-up Internet connection seemed magical. All users had to do was boot up their computers, hit a few keys on their desktop keyboards, wait for their modems to screech and scream as they established connections, and then, perhaps thirty seconds to a minute later, they were online. Checking e-mail or browsing the nascent World Wide Web was terribly slow by today's standards, but offered unprecedented convenience compared with finding information any other way. The technology was remarkable and soon became a ritual for millions of people accessing this new marvel known as the Internet.

Few of us could stand the torture of using a 2400-baud modem anymore now that we've become accustomed to our always-on, high-speed Internet connections. E-mails are now instantaneously pushed to the devices in our pockets. Our photos, music, videos, and files—not to mention the vastness of the open web—are accessible almost anywhere, anytime, on any connected device.

In line with Hauptly's assertion, as the steps required to get something done (in this case to get online and use the Internet) were removed or improved upon, adoption increased.

For example, consider the trend line of the relationship between the percentage of people creating content online and the increasing ease of doing so, as shown in figure 7.

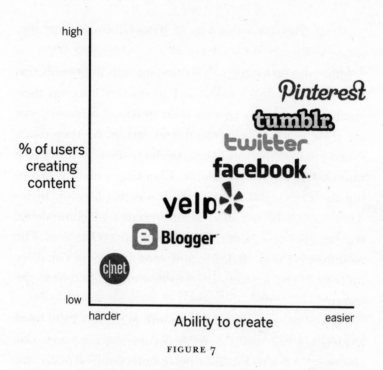

FIGURE 7

Web 1.0 was categorized by a few content providers like CNET or the *New York Times* publishing to the masses, with only a tiny number of people creating what others read.

In the late 1990s blogging changed the web. Before this era, amateur writers had to purchase their own domain, fiddle with DNS settings, find a web host, and set up a content-management system to present their writing. Suddenly, new companies such as Blogger eliminated most of these steps by allowing users to simply register an account and start posting.

Evan Williams, cofounder of Blogger, Twitter, and Medium, echoes Hauptly's formula for innovation when he describes his own approach to building three massively successful companies:

"Take a human desire, preferably one that has been around for a really long time . . . Identify that desire and use modern technology to take out steps."

Blogger made posting content online dramatically easier. The result? The percentage of users creating content online, as opposed to simply consuming it, increased.

Along came Facebook and other social media tools, refining earlier innovations such as Bulletin Board Systems (BBS) and Really Simple Syndication (RSS) feeds into tools for status update–hungry users.

Seven years after Blogger's birth, a new company described at first as a "microblogging" service sought to bring sharing to the masses: Twitter. For many, blogging was still a difficult, time-consuming venture, but anyone could type short, casual messages. *Tweeting* began to enter the national lexicon as Twitter gained wider adoption, climbing to 500 million registered users by 2012.[5] Critics first discounted Twitter's 140-character message limitation as gimmicky and restrictive; little did they realize the constraint actually increased users' ability to create. A few keyboard taps and users were sharing. As of late 2013, 340 million tweets were sent every day.

More recently, companies such as Pinterest, Instagram,

and Snapchat have elevated online content creation to a new level of simplicity. The pattern of innovation shows that making a given action easier to accomplish spurs each successive phase of the web, helping to turn the formerly niche behavior of content publishing into a mainstream habit.

As recent history of the web demonstrates, the ease or difficulty of doing a particular action affects the likelihood that a behavior will occur. To successfully simplify a product, we must remove obstacles that stand in the user's way. According to the Fogg Behavior Model, *ability is the capacity to do a particular behavior.*

ELEMENTS OF SIMPLICITY

Fogg describes six "elements of simplicity"— the factors that influence a task's difficulty.[6] These are:

- Time—how long it takes to complete an action.

- Money—the fiscal cost of taking an action.

- Physical effort—the amount of labor involved in taking the action.

- Brain cycles—the level of mental effort and focus required to take an action.

- Social deviance—how accepted the behavior is by others.

- Non-routine—according to Fogg, "How much the action matches or disrupts existing routines."

To increase the likelihood that a behavior will occur, Fogg instructs designers to focus on simplicity as a function of the user's scarcest resource at that moment. In other words: Identify what the user is missing. What is making it difficult for the user to accomplish the desired action?

Is the user short on time? Is the behavior too expensive? Is the user exhausted after a long day of work? Is the product too difficult to understand? Is the user in a social context where the behavior could be perceived as inappropriate? Is the behavior simply so far removed from the user's normal routine that its strangeness is off-putting?

These factors will differ by person and context; therefore, designers should ask, "What is the thing that is missing that would allow my users to proceed to the next step?" Designing with an eye toward simplifying the overall user experience reduces friction, removes obstacles, and helps push the user across Fogg's action line.

The action phase of the Hooked Model incorporates Fogg's six elements of simplicity by asking designers to consider how their technology can facilitate the simplest actions in anticipation of reward. The easier an action, the more likely the user is to do it and to continue the cycle through the next phase of the Hooked Model.

Below are examples of simple online interfaces used by a number of successful companies to prompt users to move quickly into the Hook's next phase.

Logging In with Facebook

Traditionally, registering for a new account with an app or Web site requires several steps. The user is prompted to enter an e-mail address, create a password, and submit other information such as a name or phone number. This burden introduces significant friction that discourages users from signing up. Mobile devices present the special challenge of smaller screens and slower typing speeds.

However, today it is nearly impossible to browse the web or use a mobile app without encountering a Facebook Login prompt (figure 8). Many companies have eliminated several steps in the registration process by enabling users to register with their sites via their existing Facebook credentials.

While the Facebook login function is useful for time-starved people, it should be noted that for others, the tool doesn't necessarily ease registration. For example, users who are wary of how Facebook might share their personal

FIGURE 8

information may not find the login button helpful because
it could trigger new anxieties (and thus, brain cycles) about
the social networking giant's trustworthiness. Again, the
roadblocks confronting users vary by person and context.
There is no "one size fits all" solution, so designers should
seek to understand an array of possible user challenges.

Sharing with the Twitter Button

Twitter helps people share articles, videos, photos, or any
other content they find on the web. The company noticed
that 25 percent of tweets contained a link and therefore
sought to make tweeting a Web site link as easy as possible.[7]

To ease the way for link sharing, Twitter created an

FIGURE 9

embeddable Tweet button for third-party sites, allowing them to offer visitors a one-click way to tweet directly from their pages (figure 9). The external trigger opens a preset message, reducing the cognitive effort of composing the tweet and saving several steps to sharing.

Searching with Google

Google, the world's most popular search engine, was not the first to market. When it launched in the late 1990s, it competed against incumbents such as Yahoo!, Lycos, Alta-Vista, and Excite. How did Google come to dominate the multibillion-dollar industry?

For starters, Google's PageRank algorithm proved to be a much more effective way to index the web. By ranking pages based on how frequently other sites linked to them, Google improved search relevancy. Compared with directory-based search tools such as Yahoo!, Google was a massive time-saver. Google also beat out other search engines that had become polluted with irrelevant content and cluttered with advertising (figure 10). From its inception, Google's clean, simple home page and search results pages were solely focused on streamlining the act of searching and getting relevant results (figure 11).

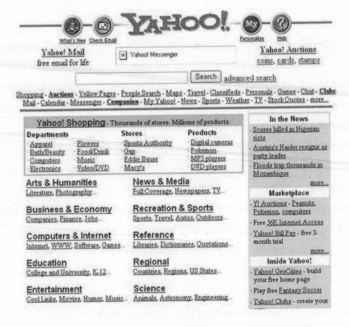

FIGURE 10—THE YAHOO! HOME PAGE, CIRCA 1998

FIGURE 11—THE GOOGLE HOME PAGE, CIRCA 1998

Simply put, Google reduced the amount of time and the cognitive effort required to find what the user was looking for. The company continues to relentlessly improve its search engine by finding new ways to remove whatever might be in the user's way—no matter how seemingly trivial. While its home page remains remarkably pristine, Google now offers myriad tools to make searching easier and faster—including automatic spelling correction, predictive results based on partial queries, and search results that load even as the user is typing. Google's efforts are intended to make searching easier to keep users coming back.

Taking Photos with the Apple iPhone

Many of life's most treasured moments come and go in an instant. We try to capture these memories in photos, but if our camera is out of reach or too cumbersome to catch the shot, we lose those moments forever. Apple recognized it could help iPhone owners take more photos by making the process easier. The company made the camera app directly launchable from the locked screen, without requiring a password. Compared with the number of steps needed to access photo apps on other smartphones at the time, the simple flick gesture of the native iPhone camera gives it a virtual monopoly as users' go-to solution whenever they need to snap a quick pic (figure 12).

FIGURE 12

Scrolling with Pinterest

How can a Web site make browsing easier? One solution, popularized by digital pin-board site Pinterest, is the infinite scroll. In the past getting from one web page to the next required clicking and waiting. However, on sites such as Pinterest, whenever the user nears the bottom of a page, more results automatically load. Users never have to pause as they continue scrolling through pins or posts without end (figure 13).

The examples above show how simplicity increases the intended user behaviors.

FIGURE 13

MOTIVATION OR ABILITY: WHICH SHOULD YOU INCREASE FIRST?

After uncovering the triggers that prompt user actions and deciding which actions you want to turn into habits, you can increase motivation and ability to spark the likelihood of your users taking a desired behavior. But which should you invest in first, motivation or ability? Where is your time and money better spent? The answer is always to start with ability.

Naturally, all three parts of B = MAT must be present for a singular user action to occur; without a clear trigger and sufficient motivation there will be no behavior. However, for companies building technology solutions, the greatest return on investment generally comes from increasing a product's ease of use.

The fact is, increasing motivation is expensive and time consuming. Web site visitors tend to ignore instructional text; they are often multitasking and have little patience for explanations about why or how they should do something. Influencing behavior by reducing the effort required to perform an action is more effective than increasing someone's desire to do it. Make your product so simple that users already know how to use it, and you've got a winner.

The Evolution of Twitter's Home Page

In 2009 the Twitter home page was cluttered with text and dozens of links (figure 14). The page was confusing, especially for new users unfamiliar with the product. Twitter's value proposition of sharing what you were doing with friends and family failed to resonate with most users, who wondered, "Why would I want to broadcast my activities?" The page design demanded a high level of attention and comprehension.

The following year Twitter redesigned its home page, touting itself as a service to "share and discover what's happening" (figure 15). Although the page became more focused

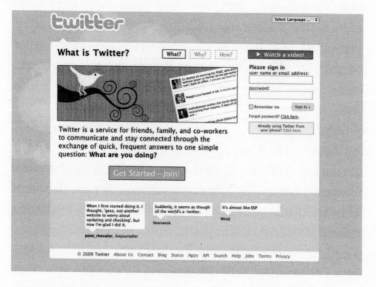

FIGURE 14—THE TWITTER HOME PAGE IN 2009

FIGURE 15—THE TWITTER HOME PAGE IN 2010

on action, it was still visually onerous. Even more unfortunate, the task users were most likely to do—search—was not
what Twitter really wanted them to do. Twitter management
knew from early users that those who followed other people
on the service were more likely to stay engaged and form a
habit. Because searching on Twitter was not helping that
goal, the company decided to make another switch.

During the company's period of hyper-growth, the Twitter home page became radically simpler (figure 16). The
product description is itself only 140 characters long and
has evolved from the cognitively difficult request that users
broadcast their information (as seen in 2009) to the less
taxing "find out what's happening, right now, with the
people and organizations you care about."

The big, bold image of people looking into some kind
of light-emanating event, like a concert or a soccer match,

FIGURE 16—THE TWITTER HOME PAGE IN 2012

metaphorically communicates the value of the service while piquing curiosity. Most strikingly, the page has two very clear calls to action: sign in or sign up. The company made the desired action as simple as possible, knowing that getting users to experience the service would yield better results than trying to persuade them to use it while still on the home page.

It is naturally worth noting that Twitter was in a different place in 2012 than in 2009. People came to the site having heard more about the service as its popularity grew. Twitter's home page evolution reveals how the company discovered its users' scarcest resource. In 2009 the Twitter home page attempted to boost motivation; by 2012 Twitter had discovered that no matter how much users knew about the service, driving them to open an account and start following people resulted in much higher engagement.

On Heuristics and Perception

We have thus far discussed Fogg's Core Motivators and the six elements of simplicity as levers for influencing the likelihood of a particular behavior occurring. These factors echo ideals of how people react when making rational decisions. For example, every Economics 101 student learns that as prices decrease, consumers purchase more—in Fogg's terms, an example of increasing ability by decreasing price.

However, although the principle seems elementary, the law, like many other theories of human behavior, has exceptions. The field of behavioral economics, as studied by luminaries such as Nobel Prize winner Daniel Kahneman, exposed exceptions to the rational model of human behavior. Even the notion that people always consume more if something costs less is a tendency, not an absolute.

There are many counterintuitive and surprising ways companies can boost users' motivation or increase their ability by understanding heuristics—*the mental shortcuts we take to make decisions and form opinions.*

It is worth mentioning four of these brain biases in particular. Even though users are often unaware of these influences on their behavior, heuristics can predict their actions.

The Scarcity Effect

In 1975 researchers Stephen Worchel, Jerry Lee, and Akanbi Adewole wanted to know how people would value cookies in two identical glass jars.[8] One jar held ten cookies while the other contained just two. Which cookies would people value more?

Although the cookies and jars were identical, participants valued the ones in the near-empty jar more highly.

The appearance of scarcity affected their perception of value.

There are many theories as to why this is the case. Scarcity may signal something about the product. If there are fewer of an item, the thinking goes, it might be because other people know something you don't—namely, that the cookies in the almost-empty jar are the better choice. The jar with just two cookies left in it conveys valuable albeit irrelevant information, because the cookies are in fact identical. Yet the perception of scarcity changed their perceived value.

In the second part of their experiment, the researchers wanted to know what would happen to the perception of the value of the cookies if they suddenly became scarce or abundant. Groups of study participants were given jars with either two cookies or ten. The people in the group with ten cookies then suddenly had eight taken away. Conversely, those with only two cookies had eight new ones added to

their jars. How would these changes affect the way participants valued the cookies?

Results remained consistent with the scarcity heuristic.
The group left with only two cookies rated them to be more
valuable, while those experiencing sudden abundance by
going from two to ten actually valued the cookies less. In
fact, they valued the cookies even lower than people who
had started with ten cookies to begin with. The study
showed that a product can decrease in perceived value if it
starts off as scarce and becomes abundant.

For an example of how perception of a limited supply
can increase sales, look no further than Amazon.com. My
recent search for a DVD revealed there were "only 14 left in
stock" (figure 17), while a search for a book I've had my eye
on says only three copies remain. Is the world's largest online retailer almost sold out of nearly everything I want to
buy or are they using the scarcity heuristic to influence my
buying behavior?

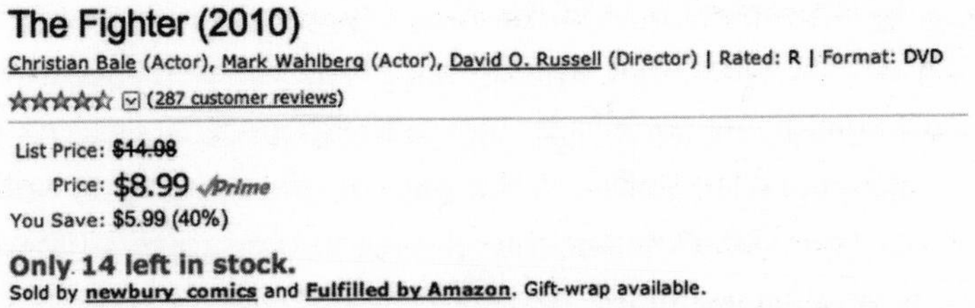

The Fighter (2010)
Christian Bale (Actor), Mark Wahlberg (Actor), David O. Russell (Director) | Rated: R | Format: DVD
★★★★☆ ☑ (287 customer reviews)

List Price: $14.98
    Price: $8.99 ✓Prime
You Save: $5.99 (40%)

Only 14 left in stock.
Sold by newbury_comics and Fulfilled by Amazon. Gift-wrap available.

FIGURE 17—"ONLY FOURTEEN LEFT IN STOCK"?

The Framing Effect

Context also shapes perception. In a social experiment, world-class violinist Joshua Bell decided to play a free impromptu concert in a Washington, D.C., subway station.[9] Bell regularly sells out venues such as the Kennedy Center and Carnegie Hall for hundreds of dollars per ticket, but when placed in the context of the D.C. subway, his music fell upon deaf ears. Almost nobody knew they were walking past one of the most talented musicians in the world.

The mind takes shortcuts informed by our surroundings to make quick and sometimes erroneous judgments.

When Bell performed his concert in the subway station, few stopped to listen. But when framed in the context of a concert hall, he can charge beaucoup bucks.

The framing heuristic not only influences our behaviors; it literally changes how our brain perceives pleasure. For example, a 2007 study attempted to measure if price had any influence on the taste of wine.[10] The researchers had study participants sample wine while in a functional magnetic resonance imaging (fMRI) machine.

As the fMRI machine scanned the blood flow in the various regions of their brains, the tasters were informed of the cost of each wine sampled. The sample started with a $5 wine and progressed to a $90 bottle. Interestingly, as the price of the wine increased, so did the participants' enjoyment of the wine. Not only did they say they enjoyed the wine more but their brain corroborated their feelings, showing higher spikes in the regions associated with pleasure. Little did the study participants realize that they were tasting the same wine each time. This study demonstrates how perception can form a personal reality based on how a product is framed, even when there is little relationship with objective quality.

The Anchoring Effect

Rarely can you walk into a clothing store without seeing signage for "30% off," "buy one, get one free," and other sales and deals. In reality these items are often marketed to maximize profits for the business. The same store often has similar but less expensive (yet not discounted) products. I recently visited a store that offered a package of three Jockey brand undershirts at a "buy one, get one half-off" discount for $29.50. After surveying other options I noticed a package of five Fruit of the Loom brand undershirts selling for $34. After doing some quick math I discovered that the undershirts not on sale were actually cheaper per shirt than the discounted brand's package.

People often anchor to one piece of information when making a decision.

I almost bought the shirts on sale assuming that the one feature differentiating the two brands—the fact that one was on sale and the other was not—was all I needed to consider.

The Endowed Progress Effect

Punch cards are often used by retailers to encourage repeat business. With each purchase customers get closer to receiving a free product or service. These cards are typically awarded empty; in effect customers start at 0 percent complete. What would happen if retailers handed customers punch cards with punches already given? Would people be more likely to take action if they had already made some progress? An experiment sought to answer this very question.[11]

Two groups of customers were given punch cards awarding a free car wash once the cards were fully punched. One group was given a blank punch card with eight squares; the other was given a punch card with ten squares that came with two free punches. Both groups still had to purchase eight car washes to receive a free wash; however, the second group of customers—those that were given two free punches—had a staggering 82 percent higher completion rate.

The study demonstrates the endowed progress effect, a phenomenon that increases motivation as people believe they are nearing a goal.

Sites such as LinkedIn and Facebook utilize this heuristic to encourage people to divulge more information about

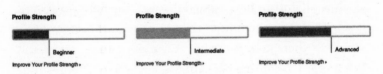

FIGURE 18

themselves when completing their online profiles. On LinkedIn every user starts with some semblance of progress (figure 18). The next step is to "Improve Your Profile Strength" by supplying additional information. As users complete each step, the meter incrementally shows the user is advancing. Cleverly, LinkedIn's completion bar jump-starts the perception of progress and does not include a numeric scale. For the new user, a proper LinkedIn profile does not seem so far away. Yet even the "advanced" user still has additional steps she can take to inch toward the final goal.

Most people remain unaware of how heuristics help us make split-second decisions multiple times per day. Psychologists believe there are hundreds of cognitive biases that influence our behaviors; the four discussed here are just a few examples.[12] For product designers building habit-forming technology, understanding and leveraging these methods for boosting motivation and ability can prove highly impactful.

In this chapter we discovered how to take users from trigger to action. We explored how cognitive biases influence behavior and how, by designing the simplest action in anticipation of a reward, product makers can advance users to the next phase of the Hooked Model.

Now that users have passed through the first two phases, it is time to give them what they came for—the reward that scratches their itch. But what is it exactly that users want? What keeps us coming back time and again to habit-forming experiences and technologies? The answer to what we're all searching for is the topic of the next chapter.

REMEMBER & SHARE

- The second step in the Hooked Model is *action*.

- The action is the simplest behavior in anticipation of reward.

- As described by Dr. B. J. Fogg's Behavior Model:

  - For any behavior to occur, a trigger must be present at the same time as the user has sufficient ability and motivation to take action.

  - To increase the desired behavior, ensure a clear trigger is present; next, increase ability by making the action easier to do; finally, align with the right motivator.

  - Every behavior is driven by one of three Core Motivators: seeking pleasure and avoiding pain; seeking hope and avoiding fear; seeking social acceptance while avoiding social rejection.

- Ability is influenced by the six factors of time, money, physical effort, brain cycles, social deviance, and non-routineness. Ability is dependent on users and their context at that moment.

- *Heuristics* are cognitive shortcuts we take to make quick decisions. Product designers can utilize many of the hundreds of heuristics to increase the likelihood of their desired action.

DO THIS NOW

Refer to the answers you came up with in the last "Do This Now" section to complete the following exercises:

- Walk through the path your users would take to use your product or service, beginning from the time they feel their internal trigger to the point where they receive their expected outcome. How many steps does it take before users obtain the reward they came for? How does this process compare with the simplicity of some of the examples described in this chapter? How does it compare with competing products and services?

- Which resources are limiting your users' ability to accomplish the tasks that will become habits?

- Time

- Brain cycles (too confusing)

- Money

- Social deviance (outside the norm)

- Physical effort

- Non-routine (too new)

- Brainstorm three testable ways to make intended tasks easier to complete.

- Consider how you might apply heuristics to make habit-forming actions more likely.

Reward

| 4 |

Variable Reward

Ultimately, all businesses help users achieve an objective. As we learned in the previous chapter, reducing the steps needed to complete the intended outcome increases the likelihood of that outcome. But to keep users engaged, products need to deliver on their promises. To form the learned associations we discussed in chapter 2, the trigger phase, users must come to depend on the product as a reliable solution to their problem—the salve for the itch they came to scratch.

The third step in the Hooked Model is the *variable reward phase*, in which you reward your users by solving a problem, reinforcing their motivation for the action taken in the previous phase. To understand why rewards—and variable rewards in particular—are so powerful, we must first take a trip deep inside the brain.

Understanding Rewards

In the 1940s two researchers, James Olds and Peter Milner, accidentally discovered how a special area of the brain is the source of our cravings. The researchers implanted electrodes in the brains of lab mice that enabled the mice to give themselves tiny electric shocks to a small area of the brain, the nucleus accumbens.[1] The mice quickly became hooked on the sensation.

Olds and Milner demonstrated that the lab mice would forgo food, water, and even run across a painful electrified grid for the opportunity to continue pressing the lever that administered the shocks. A few years later, other researchers tested the human response to self-administered stimulus in the same area of the brain. The results were just as dramatic as in the mouse trial—subjects wanted to do nothing but press the brain-stimulating button. Even when the machine was turned off, people continued pressing the button. Researchers had to forcibly take the devices from subjects who refused to relinquish them.

Given the responses they had earlier found in lab animals, Olds and Milner concluded that they had discovered the brain's pleasure center. In fact, we now know other things that feel good also activate the same neural region. Sex, delicious food, a bargain, and even our digital devices all tap into this deep recess of the brain, providing the impetus for many of our behaviors.

However, more recent research has shown that these two researchers' experiments were not stimulating pleasure per se. Stanford professor Brian Knutson conducted a study exploring blood flow in the brains of people wagering while inside an fMRI machine.[2] The test subjects played a gambling game while Knutson and his team looked at which areas of their brains became more active. The startling results showed that the nucleus accumbens was not activating when the reward (in this case a monetary payout) was received, but rather in anticipation of it.

> *The study revealed that what draws us to act is not the sensation we receive from the reward itself, but the need to alleviate the craving for that reward.*

The stress of desire in the brain appears to compel us, just as it did in Olds's and Milner's lab mouse experiments.

UNDERSTANDING VARIABILITY

If you've never watched a YouTube video of a baby's first encounter with a dog, it's worth doing. Not only are these videos incredibly cute, but they help demonstrate something important about our mental wiring.

At first the expression on the baby's face seems to ask, "What is this hairy monster doing in my house? Will it hurt me? What will it do next?" The child is filled with curiosity, uncertain if this creature might cause harm. But soon the child figures out Rover is not a threat. What follows is an explosion of infectious giggles. Researchers believe laughter may in fact be a release valve when we experience the discomfort and excitement of uncertainty, but without fear of harm.[3]

What we do not see in the videos is what happens over time. A few years later, what was once thrilling about Rover no longer holds the child's attention in the same way. The child has learned to predict the dog's behavior and no longer finds the pup quite as entertaining. By now, the child's mind is occupied with dump trucks, fire engines, bicycles, and new toys that stimulate the senses—until they too become predictable. Without variability we are like children in that once we figure out what will happen next, we become less excited by the experience. The same rules that apply to puppies also apply to products. To hold our attention, products must have an ongoing degree of novelty.

Our brains have evolved over millennia to help us figure out how things work. Once we understand causal relationships, we retain that information in memory. Our habits are simply the brain's ability to quickly retrieve the appropriate behavioral response to a routine or process we have already learned. Habits help us conserve our attention for other things while we go about the tasks we perform with little or no conscious thought.

However, when something breaks the cause-and-effect pattern we've come to expect—when we encounter something outside the norm—we suddenly become aware of it again.[4] Novelty sparks our interest, makes us pay attention, and—like a baby encountering a friendly dog for the first time—we seem to love it.

Rewards of the Tribe, the Hunt, and the Self

In the 1950s psychologist B. F. Skinner conducted experiments to understand how variability impacted animal behavior.[5] First, Skinner placed hungry pigeons inside a box rigged to deliver a food pellet to the birds every time they pressed a lever. Similar to Olds's and Milner's lab mice, the pigeons learned the cause-and-effect relationship between pressing the lever and receiving the food.

In the next part of the experiment Skinner added variability. Instead of providing a pellet every time a pigeon tapped the lever, the machine discharged food after a random number of taps. Sometimes the lever dispensed food, other times not. Skinner revealed that the intermittent reward dramatically increased the number of times the pigeons tapped the lever. Adding variability increased the frequency of the pigeons' completing the intended action.

Skinner's pigeons tell us a great deal about what helps drive our own behaviors. More recent experiments reveal that variability increases activity in the nucleus accumbens and spikes levels of the neurotransmitter dopamine, driving our hungry search for rewards.[6] Researchers observed increased dopamine levels in the nucleus accumbens in experiments involving monetary rewards as well as in a study of heterosexual men viewing images of attractive women's faces.[7]

Variable rewards can be found in all sorts of products

and experiences that hold our attention. They fuel our drive to check e-mail, browse the web, or bargain-shop. I propose that variable rewards come in three types: *the tribe, the hunt,* and *the self.* Habit-forming products utilize one or more of these variable reward types.

Rewards of the Tribe

We are a species that depends on one another. Rewards of the tribe, or social rewards, are driven by our connectedness with other people.

> *Our brains are adapted to seek rewards that make us feel accepted, attractive, important, and included.*

Many of our institutions and industries are built around this need for social reinforcement. From civic and religious groups to spectator sports and "watercooler" television shows, the need to feel social connectedness shapes our values and drives much of how we spend our time.

It is no surprise that social media has exploded in popularity. Facebook, Twitter, Pinterest, and several other sites collectively provide over a billion people with powerful social rewards on a variable schedule. With every post, tweet, or pin, users anticipate social validation. Rewards of the tribe keep users coming back, wanting more.

Sites that leverage tribal rewards benefit from what psychologist Albert Bandura called "social learning theory."[8] Bandura studied the power of modeling and ascribed special powers to our ability to learn from others. In particular Bandura determined that people who observe someone being rewarded for a particular behavior are more likely to alter their own beliefs and subsequent actions. Notably, Bandura also demonstrated that this technique works particularly well when people observe the behavior of people most like themselves or who are slightly more experienced (and therefore, role models).[9] This is exactly the kind of targeted demographic and interest-level segmentation that social media companies such as Facebook and industry-specific sites such as Stack Overflow selectively apply.

Here are some online examples of rewards of the tribe:

1. FACEBOOK

Facebook provides numerous examples of variable social rewards. Logging in reveals an endless stream of content friends have shared, comments from others, and running tallies of how many people have "liked" something. The uncertainty of what users will find each time they visit the site creates the intrigue needed to pull them back again.

While variable content gets users to keep searching for interesting tidbits in their News Feeds, a click of the "Like" button provides a variable reward for the content's creators. "Likes" and comments offer tribal validation for those who shared the content, and provide variable rewards that motivate them to continue posting.

2. STACK OVERFLOW

Stack Overflow is the world's largest question-and-answer site for software developers. As with other user-generated content sites such as Quora, Wikipedia, and YouTube, all of Stack Overflow's content is created voluntarily by people who use the site. A staggering five thousand answers to questions are generated per day by site members. Many of these responses provide detailed, highly technical and time-consuming answers. But why do so many people spend so much time doing all this work for free? What motivates them to invest the effort into what others may see as the burdensome task of writing technical documentation?

Stack Overflow devotees write responses in anticipation of rewards of the tribe. Each time a user submits an answer, other members have the opportunity to vote the response up or down. The best responses percolate upward, accumulating points for their authors (figure 19). When they reach certain point levels, members earn badges, which confer special status and privileges. Naturally, the process of accumulating upvotes is highly variable—no one knows how many will be received from the community when responding to a question.

Stack Overflow works because, like all of us, software engineers find satisfaction in contributing to a community they care about. The element of variability also turns a seemingly mundane task into an engaging, gamelike experience. Yet on Stack Overflow, points are not just an empty game mechanic; they confer special value by repre-

FIGURE 19

senting how much someone has contributed to his or her tribe. Users enjoy the feeling of helping their fellow programmers and earning the respect of people whose opinions they value.

3. LEAGUE OF LEGENDS

League of Legends, a popular computer game, launched in 2009 and quickly achieved tremendous success. Soon after its launch, however, the game's owners found they had a serious problem: The online video game was filled with "trolls"—people who enjoyed bullying other players while being protected by the anonymity the game provides. *League of Legends* soon earned a nasty reputation for having an "unforgiving—even abusive—community."[10] A leading industry publication wrote, "*League of Legends* has become well known for at least two things: proving the power of the free-to-play model in the West and a vicious player community."[11]

To combat the trolls, the game creators designed a reward system leveraging Bandura's social learning theory, which they called Honor Points (figure 20). The system gave players the ability to award points for particularly sportsmanlike conduct worthy of recognition. These virtual kudos encouraged positive behavior and helped the best and most cooperative players to stand out in the community. The number of points earned was highly variable and could only be conferred by other players. Honor Points soon became a coveted marker of tribe-conferred status and helped weed out trolls by signaling to others which players should be avoided.

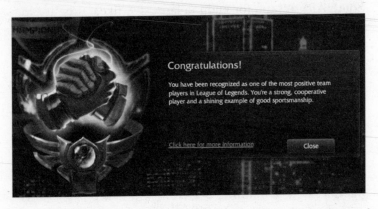

FIGURE 20

Rewards of the Hunt

For years, scientists have tried to answer a central question of human evolution: How did early humans hunt for food? Most evolutionary biologists agree that consuming animal protein was a significant milestone that led to better nutrition and, ultimately, bigger brains; however, the tactical details of the hunt remain hazy.[12] We know our ancestors handcrafted spears and arrows for hunting, but evidence shows that these weapons were only invented five hundred thousand years ago,[13] whereas we've been eating meat for over 2 million years.[14] How, then, did we hunt during the first 75 percent of our existence?

According to Harvard evolutionary biologist Daniel Lieberman, we chased down our dinner. Early humans killed animals using a technique known as "persistence hunting," a practice still common among today's few remaining pre-agrarian societies. One of these groups, the San people of South Africa, hunt for kudu (a large deerlike animal) using a technique similar to the way Lieberman believes humans hunted for the vast majority of our species' history. The way we evolved to hunt wild game may help explain why we feel compelled to use certain products today.

In Africa the chase begins when a group of San hunters separate a large kudu bull from the herd. The animal's heavy antlers slow him down, making him less agile than the female kudus. Once the animal is isolated from the pack, a single San hunter begins the hunt, keeping a steady pace as the animal leaps ahead in fear. At first it appears the man will never catch up to the bounding beast. At times he struggles to keep the animal in sight through the dry brush.

Yet the hunter knows he can use the animal's weaknesses to his advantage. The powerful kudu is much faster in short sprints, but the kudu's skin is covered with fur and cannot dissipate heat like the runner's skin can. According to Lieberman, "Quadrupeds cannot pant and gallop at the same time."[15] When the kudu must stop to catch his breath, the hunter begins closing in, not to catch it but to run it to exhaustion.

After being tracked for a sweltering eight hours under the African sun, the beast is finally ready to give up, collapsing in surrender with barely a struggle. The meager hundred-pound San hunter outlasts the powerful five-hundred-pound beast with little more than his persistence and the biomechanical gifts evolution has given him. The hunter swiftly and ceremoniously kills his prize, piercing a vein in the animal's neck so that he can feed his children and his tribe.

By running on two feet and lacking the body hair typical of other primates, our species gained a massive advantage over larger mammals. Our ability to maintain steady pursuit gave us the capacity to hunt large prehistoric game. Yet persistence hunting was not only made possible because of our bodies; changes in our brains also played a significant role.

During the chase, the runner is driven by the pursuit itself; this same mental hardwiring also provides clues into the source of our insatiable desires today. The dogged determination that keeps San hunters chasing kudu is the same mechanism that keeps us wanting and buying. Although it is a long way from bushmen to businessmen, the mental processes of the hunt remain largely the same.

The search for resources defines the next type of variable reward—the rewards of the hunt.

The need to acquire physical objects, such as food and other supplies that aid our survival, is part of our brain's operating system.

Where we once hunted for food, today we hunt for other things. In modern society, food can be bought with cash, and more recently by extension, information translates into money.

Rewards of the hunt existed long before the advent of computers. Yet today we find numerous examples of variable rewards associated with the pursuit of resources and information that compel us with the same determination as the San hunter chasing his prey.

Here are a few examples of products that create habits by leveraging rewards of the hunt:

1. MACHINE GAMBLING

Most people know that gambling benefits the casino or broker far more than the players. As the old adage says,

"The house always wins." Yet despite this knowledge, the
multibillion-dollar gambling industry continues to thrive.

Slot machines provide a classic example of variable rewards of the hunt. Gamblers plunk $1 billion per day into
slot machines in American casinos, which is a testament to
the machines' power to compel players.[16] By awarding
money in random intervals, games of chance entice players
with the prospect of a jackpot. Naturally, winning is entirely
outside the gambler's control—yet the pursuit can be in-
toxicating.

2. TWITTER

The "feed" has become a social staple of many online products. The stream of limitless information displayed in a
scrolling interface makes for a compelling reward of the
hunt. The Twitter timeline, for example, is filled with a mix
of both mundane and relevant content. This variety creates an enticingly unpredictable user experience. On occasion a user might find a particularly interesting piece of
news, while other times she won't. To keep hunting for
more information, all that is needed is a flick of the finger
or scroll of a mouse. Users scroll and scroll and scroll to
search for variable rewards in the form of relevant tweets
(figure 21).

FIGURE 21

3. PINTEREST

Pinterest, a company that has grown to reach over 250 million monthly users worldwide, also employs a feed, but with a visual twist.[17] The online pinboarding site is a virtual smorgasbord of objects of desire. The site is curated by its community of users who ensure that a high degree of intriguing content appears on each page.

FIGURE 22

Pinterest users never know what they will find on the site. To keep them searching and scrolling, the company employs an unusual design. As the user scrolls to the bottom of the page, some images appear to be cut off. Images often appear out of view below the browser fold. However, these images offer a glimpse of what's ahead, even if just barely visible. To relieve their curiosity, all users have to do is scroll to reveal the full picture (figure 22). As more images load on the page, the endless search for variable rewards of the hunt continues.

Rewards of the Self

Finally, there are the variable rewards we seek for a more personal form of gratification. We are driven to conquer obstacles, even if just for the satisfaction of doing so. Pursuing a task to completion can influence people to continue all sorts of behaviors.[18] Surprisingly, we even pursue these rewards when we don't outwardly appear to enjoy them. For example, watching someone investing countless hours into completing a tabletop puzzle can reveal frustrated face contortions and even sounds of muttered profanity. Although puzzles offer no prize other than the satisfaction of completion, for some the painstaking search for the right pieces can be a wonderfully mesmerizing struggle.

The rewards of the self are fueled by "intrinsic motivation" as highlighted by the work of Edward Deci and Richard Ryan. Their self-determination theory espouses that people desire, among other things, to gain a sense of competency. Adding an element of mystery to this goal makes the pursuit all the more enticing.[19]

The experiences below offer examples of variable rewards of the self.

1. VIDEO GAMES

Rewards of the self are a defining component in video games, as players seek to master the skills needed to pursue their quest. Leveling up, unlocking special powers, and other game mechanics fulfill a player's desire for competency by showing progression and completion.

For example, advancing a character through the popular online game *World of Warcraft* unlocks new abilities

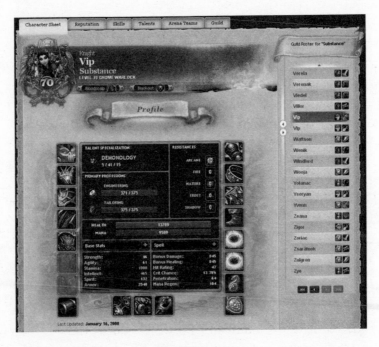

FIGURE 23

for the player (figure 23). The thirst to acquire advanced
weaponry, visit uncharted lands, and improve their characters' scores motivates players to invest more hours in the
game.

2. E-MAIL

You do not have to be a hard-core video gamer to be
heavily influenced by gamelike experiences. The humble
e-mail system provides an example of how the search for

mastery, completion, and competence moves users to habitual and sometimes mindless actions. Have you ever caught yourself checking your e-mail for no particular reason? Perhaps you unconsciously decided to open it to see what messages might be waiting for you. For many, the number of unread messages represents a sort of goal to be completed.

Yet to feel rewarded, the user must have a sense of accomplishment. What happens when in-boxes become flooded with too many messages? Users can give up when they sense the struggle to get their in-boxes under control is hopeless. To combat the problem and give users a sense of progress, Google created "Priority Inbox."[20] Using this feature, Gmail cleverly segments e-mails into sorted folders to increase the frequency of users achieving "in-box zero"—a near-mystical state of having no unread e-mails. Of course, some of the folder sorting is done through digital sleight-of-hand by pushing some low priority e-mails out of sight. However, by giving users the sense that they are processing their in-box more efficiently, Gmail delivers a feeling of completion and mastery.

3. CODECADEMY

Learning to program is not easy. Software engineers take months, if not years, of diligent hard work before they have the confidence and skill to write useful code. Many people attempt to learn how to write software only to give up, frustrated at the tedious process of learning a new computer language.

Codecademy seeks to make learning to write code more fun and rewarding. The site offers step-by-step instructions for building a web app, animation, and even a browser-based game. The interactive lessons deliver immediate feedback, in contrast to traditional methods of learning to code by writing whole programs. At Codecademy users can enter a single correct function and the code works or doesn't, providing instant feedback.

Learning a new skill is often filled with errors but Codecademy uses the difficulty to its advantage. There is a constant element of the unknown when it comes to completing the task at hand; like in a game, users receive variable rewards as they learn—sometimes they succeed, sometimes they fail. Yet as their competency level improves, users work to advance through levels, mastering the curriculum. Codecademy's symbols of progression and instantaneous variable feedback tap into rewards of the self, turning a difficult path into an engaging challenge (figure 24).

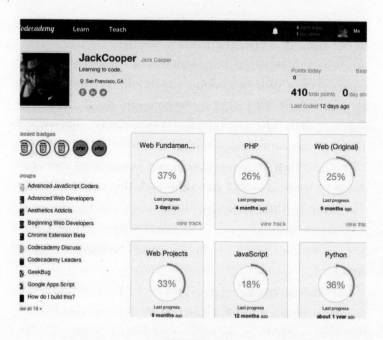

FIGURE 24

Important Considerations for Designing Reward Systems

Variable Rewards Are Not a Free Pass

In May 2007 a Web site named Mahalo.com was born. A flagship feature of the new site was a question-and-answer forum, "Mahalo Answers." Unlike previous Q&A sites, Mahalo utilized a special incentive to get users to ask and answer questions.

First, people who submitted a question offered a bounty in the form of a virtual currency, "Mahalo Dollars." Next, other users contributed answers to the question; the best response received the bounty, which could be exchanged for real money. By providing a monetary reward, the Mahalo founders believed they could drive user engagement and form new online user habits.

At first Mahalo garnered significant attention and traffic. At its high point 14.1 million users worldwide visited the site monthly.[21] But over time, users began to lose interest. Although the payout of the bounties was variable, somehow users did not find the monetary rewards enticing enough.

As Mahalo struggled to retain users, another Q&A site began to boom. Quora, launched in 2010 by two former Facebook employees, quickly grew in popularity. Unlike Mahalo, Quora did not offer a single cent to anyone answering user questions. Why, then, have users remained highly engaged with Quora but not with Mahalo, despite its variable monetary rewards?

In Mahalo's case, executives assumed that paying users would drive repeat engagement with the site. After all, people like money, right? Unfortunately, Mahalo had an incomplete understanding of its users' drivers.

Ultimately, the company found that people did not want to use a Q&A site to make money. If the trigger was a desire for monetary rewards, users were better off spending their time earning an hourly wage. And if the payouts were meant to take the form of a game, like a slot machine, then the rewards came far too infrequently and were too small to matter.

However, Quora demonstrated that social rewards and the variable reinforcement of recognition from peers proved to be much more frequent and salient motivators. Quora instituted an upvoting system that reports user satisfaction with answers and provides a steady stream of social feedback. Quora's social rewards have proven more attractive than Mahalo's monetary rewards.

Only by understanding what truly matters to users can a company correctly match the right variable reward to their intended behavior.

Recently, *gamification*—defined as the use of gamelike elements in nongame environments—has been used with varying success. Points, badges, and leaderboards can prove effective, but only if they scratch the user's itch. When there is a mismatch between the customer's problem and the company's assumed solution, no amount of gamification will help spur engagement. Likewise, if the user has no ongoing itch at all—say, no need to return repeatedly to a site that lacks any value beyond the initial visit—gamification will fail because of a lack of inherent interest in the product or service offered. In other words, gamification is not a "one size fits all" solution for driving user engagement.

Variable rewards are not magic fairy dust that a product

designer can sprinkle onto a product to make it instantly more attractive. Rewards must fit into the narrative of *why* the product is used and align with the user's internal triggers and motivations. They must ultimately improve the user's life.

Maintain a Sense of Autonomy

Quora found success by connecting the right reward to the intended behavior of asking and answering questions. In August 2012, though, the company committed a very public blunder—one that illustrates another important consideration when using variable rewards.

In an effort to increase user engagement, Quora introduced a new feature, "Views," which revealed the real identity of people visiting a particular question or answer. For users, the idea of knowing who was seeing content they added to the site proved very intriguing. Users could now know, for example, when a celebrity or prominent venture capital investor viewed something they created.

However, the feature backfired. Quora automatically opted users in to the new feature without alerting them that their browsing history on the site would be exposed to others. In an instant, users lost their treasured anonymity when asking, answering, or simply viewing Quora questions that were personal, awkward, or intimate.[22] The move sparked a user revolt and Quora reversed course a few weeks later, making the feature explicitly opt-in.[23]

In this case the change felt forced and bordered on co-ercion. Although influencing behavior can be a part of good product design, heavy-handed efforts may have ad-verse consequences and risk losing users' trust.

We'll address the morality of manipulation in a later chapter—but aside from the ethical considerations, there is an important point regarding the psychological role of au-tonomy and how it can impact user engagement.

As part of a French study, researchers wanted to know if they could influence how much money people handed to a total stranger asking for bus fare by using just a few spe-cially encoded words. They discovered a technique so simple and effective it doubled the amount people gave.

The turn of phrase has not only proven to increase how much bus fare people give, but has also been effective in boosting charitable donations and participation in volun-tary surveys. In fact, a recent meta-analysis of forty-two studies involving over twenty-two thousand participants concluded that these few words, placed at the end of a re-quest, are a highly effective way to gain compliance, dou-bling the likelihood of people saying yes.[24]

The magic words the researchers discovered? The phrase "But you are free to accept or refuse."

The "but you are free" technique demonstrates how we are more likely to be persuaded to give when our ability to choose is reaffirmed. Not only was the effect observed during face-to-face interactions, but also over e-mail. Although the re-search did not directly look at how products and services might use the technique, the study provides an important insight into how companies maintain or lose the user's attention.

Why does reminding people of their freedom to choose, as demonstrated in the French bus fare study, prove so effective?

The researchers believe the phrase "But you are free" disarms our instinctive rejection of being told what to do. If you have ever grumbled at your mother when she tells you to put on a coat or felt your blood pressure rise when your boss micromanages you, you have experienced what psychologists term *reactance*, the hair-trigger response to threats to your autonomy.

However, when a request is coupled with an affirmation of the right to choose, reactance is kept at bay. Yet can the principles of autonomy and reactance carry over into the way products change user behavior and drive the formation of new user habits? Here are two examples to make the case that they do—but naturally, you are free to make up your own mind.

Establishing the habit of better nutrition is a common goal for many Americans. Searching in the Apple App Store for the word *diet* returns 3,235 apps that all promise to help users shed extra pounds. The first app in the long list is MyFitnessPal, whose iOS app is rated by over 350,000 people.

A year ago when I decided to lose a few pounds, I installed the app and gave it a try. MyFitnessPal is simple enough to use. The app asked me to log what I ate and presented me with a calorie score based on my weight-loss goal.

For a few days I stuck with the program and diligently input information about everything I ate. Had I been a person who had previously logged food using pen and paper, MyFitnessPal would have been a welcome improvement.

However, I was not a calorie tracker prior to using My-FitnessPal and although using the app was novel at first, it soon became a drag. Keeping a food diary was not part of my daily routine and was not something I came to the app wanting to do. I wanted to lose weight and the app was telling me how to do it with its strict method of tracking calories in and calories out. Unfortunately, I soon found that forgetting to enter a meal made it impossible to get back on the program—the rest of my day was a nutritional wash.

I soon began to feel obligated to confess my mealtime transgressions to my phone. MyFitnessPal became MyFitnessPain. Yes, I had chosen to install the app at first, but despite my best intentions, my motivation faded and using the app became a chore. Adopting a weird new behavior—calorie tracking, in my case—felt like something I had to do, not something I wanted to do. My only options were to comply or quit; I chose the latter.

On the other hand Fitocracy, another health app, approaches behavior change very differently. The goal of the app is similar to its competitors—to help people establish better diet and exercise routines. However, it leverages familiar behaviors users *want* to do, instead of *have* to do.

Initially, the Fitocracy experience is similar to other health apps, encouraging new members to track their food consumption and exercise. Where Fitocracy differentiates itself is in its recognition that most users will quickly fall off the wagon, just as I had with MyFitnessPal, unless the app taps into existing autonomous behavior.

Before my reactance alarm went off, I started receiving kudos from other members of the site after entering my very first run. Curious to know who was sending the virtual encouragement, I logged in, whereupon I immediately saw a question from "mrosplock5," a woman looking for advice on what to do about knee pain from running. Having experienced similar trouble several years back, I left a quick reply: "Running barefoot (or with minimalist shoes) eliminated my knee pains. Strange but true!"

I have not used Fitocracy for long, but it is easy to see how someone could get hooked. Fitocracy is first and foremost an online community. The app roped me in by closely mimicking real-world gym jabber among friends. The ritual of connecting with like-minded people existed long before Fitocracy, and the company leverages this behavior by making it easier and more rewarding to share encouragement, exchange advice, and receive praise. In fact, a recent study found social factors were the most important reasons people used the service and recommended it to others.[25]

Social acceptance is something we all crave, and Fitocracy leverages the universal need for connection as an on-ramp to fitness, making new tools and features available to users as they develop new habits. The choice for the Fitocracy user is therefore between the old way of doing an existing behavior and the company's tailored solution for easing the user into healthy new habits.

To be fair, MyFitnessPal also has social features intended to keep members engaged. However, as opposed to Fitocracy, the benefits of interacting with the community come much later in the user experience, if ever.

Clearly, it is too early to tell which among the multitudes of new wellness apps and products will emerge victorious, but the fact remains that the most successful consumer technologies—those that have altered the daily behaviors of billions of people—are the ones that nobody *makes* us use. Perhaps part of the appeal of sneaking in a few minutes on Instagram or checking scores on ESPN.com is our access to a moment of pure autonomy—an escape from being told what to do by bosses and coworkers.

Unfortunately, too many companies build their products betting users will do what they *make* them do instead of letting them do what they *want* to do. Companies fail to change user behaviors because they do not make their services enjoyable for its own sake, often asking users to learn new, unfamiliar actions instead of making old routines easier.

Companies that successfully change behaviors present users with an implicit choice between their old way of doing things and a new, more convenient way to fulfill existing needs.

By maintaining the users' freedom to choose, products can facilitate the adoption of new habits and change behavior for good.

Whether coerced into doing something we did not intend, as was the case when Quora opted in all users to its Views feature, or feeling forced to adopt a strange new calorie-counting behavior on MyFitnessPal, people often feel constrained by threats to their autonomy and rebel. To change behavior, products must ensure the users feel in control. People must want to use the service, not feel they have to.

Beware of Finite Variability

In 2008 a television show, *Breaking Bad*, began receiving unprecedented critical and popular acclaim. The show followed the life of Walter White, a high school chemistry teacher who transforms himself into a crystal meth–cooking drug lord. As the body count on the show piled up season after season, so did its viewership.[26] The first episode of the final season in 2013 attracted 5.9 million viewers and by the end of the series, *Guinness World Records* dubbed it the highest-rated TV series of all time.[27] Although *Breaking Bad* owes a great deal of its success to its talented cast and crew, fundamentally the program utilized a simple formula to keep people tuning in.

At the heart of every episode—and also across each season's narrative arc—is a problem the characters must resolve. For example, during an episode in the first season, Walter White must find a way to dispose of the bodies of two rival drug dealers. Challenges prevent resolution of the conflict and suspense is created as the audience waits to find out how the story line ends. In this particular episode White discovers one of the drug dealers is still alive and is faced with the dilemma of having to kill someone he thought was already dead. Invariably, each episode's central conflict is resolved near the end of the show, at which time a new challenge arises to pique the viewer's curiosity. By design, the only way to know how Walter gets out of the mess he is in at the end of the latest episode is to watch the next episode.

The cycle of conflict, mystery, and resolution is as old as storytelling itself, and at the heart of every good tale is variability. The unknown is fascinating, and strong stories hold our attention by waiting to reveal what happens next. In a phenomenon termed *experience-taking*, researchers have shown that people who read a story about a character actually feel what the protagonist is feeling.[28] As we step into the character's shoes we experience his or her motivations—including the search for rewards of the tribe, the hunt, and the self. We empathize with characters because they are driven by the same things that drive us.

Yet if the search to resolve uncertainty is such a powerful tool of engagement, why do we eventually lose interest in the things that once riveted us? Many people have experienced the intense focus of being hooked on a TV series, a great book, a new video game, or even the latest gadget. However, most of us lose interest in a few days' or weeks' time. Why does the power of variable rewards seem to fade away?

Perhaps no company in recent memory epitomizes the mercurial nature of variable rewards quite like Zynga, makers of the hit Facebook game *FarmVille*. In 2009 *FarmVille* undeniably became part of the global zeitgeist. The game smashed records as it quickly reached 83.8 million monthly active users by leveraging the Facebook platform to acquire new players.[29] In 2010, as "farmers" tended their digital crops while paying real money for virtual goods and levels, the company generated more than $36 million in revenue.[30]

The company seemed invincible and set a course for growth by cloning its *FarmVille* success into a franchise. Zynga soon released *CityVille*, *ChefVille*, *FrontierVille*, and several more *-Ville* titles using familiar game mechanics in the hope that people would enjoy them as voraciously as they had *FarmVille*. By March 2012 Zynga's stock was flying high and the company was valued at over $10 billion.

Yet by November of that same year, the stock was down over 80 percent. It turned out that Zynga's new games were not really new at all. The company had simply done retreads of *FarmVille*; players had lost interest and investors followed suit. What was once novel and intriguing became rote and boring. The *-Villes* had lost their variability and with it, their viability.

As the Zynga story demonstrates, an element of mystery is an important component of continued user interest. Online games like *FarmVille* suffer from what I term *finite variability*— an experience that becomes predictable after use. While *Breaking Bad* built suspense over time as the audience wondered how the series would end, eventually interest in the show waned when it finally concluded. The series enthralled viewers with each new episode, but now that it is all over, how many people who saw it once will watch it again? With the plot lines known and the central mysteries revealed, the show just won't seem as interesting the second time around. Perhaps this series might resurrect interest with a new spin-off show in the future, but viewership for old episodes people have already seen will never peak as it did when they were new.*

Experiences with finite variability become less engaging because they eventually become predictable.

Businesses with finite variability are not inferior per se; they just operate under different constraints. They must constantly churn out new content and experiences to cater to their consumers' insatiable desire for novelty. It is no coincidence that both Hollywood and the video gaming industry operate under what is called the *studio model*, whereby a deep-pocketed company provides backing and distribution to a portfolio of movies or games, uncertain which one will become the next megahit.

This is in contrast with companies making products exhibiting *infinite variability*—experiences that maintain user interest by sustaining variability with use. For example, games played to completion offer finite variability, while those played with other people have higher degrees of infinite variability

* A year after the first edition of this book was published, *Better Call Saul*, a *Breaking Bad* spin-off, did in fact air.

because the players themselves alter the gameplay throughout. *World of Warcraft*, the world's most popular massively multi-player online role-playing game, still captures the attention of more than 10 million active users eight years after its release.[31] *FarmVille* is played mostly in solitude, but *World of Warcraft* is frequently played with teams; it is the hard-to-predict behavior of other people that keeps the game interesting.

While content consumption, like watching a TV show, is an example of finite variability, content creation is infinitely variable. Sites like Dribbble, a platform for designers and artists to showcase their work, exemplify the longer-lasting engagement that comes from infinite variability. On the site contributors share their designs in search of feedback from other artists. As new trends and design patterns change, so do Dribbble's pages. The variety of what Dribbble users can create is limitless, and the constantly changing site always offers new surprises.

Platforms like YouTube, Facebook, Pinterest, and Twitter all leverage user-generated content to provide visitors with a never-ending stream of newness. Naturally, even sites utilizing infinite variability are not guaranteed to hold on to users forever. Eventually—to borrow from the title of Michael Lewis's 1999 book about the dot-com boom in Silicon Valley—the "new new thing" comes along and consumers migrate to it for the reasons discussed in earlier chapters. However, products utilizing infinite variability stand a better chance of holding on to users' attention, while those with finite variability must constantly reinvent themselves just to keep pace.

Inherent Variability

While some products, like the ones we've just discussed, add variability to the user experience, others operate in conditions that are already variable. For example, Google wouldn't want to add variability to its search results page because searching on the web is inherently variable. Uber wouldn't want to add variability to your ride because the experience of getting to where you're going is already plagued with uncertainty—"Will I get to where I'm going on time?"

For companies like Google and Uber, adding more variability to an inherently variable user experience makes no sense. Can you imagine what would happen if your Uber driver decided to take you for a spin around the block just for fun?

Remember, variability is only engaging when the user maintains a sense of autonomy. People will stand in line for hours to ride the twists and turns of a roller coaster but are panic stricken when they experience a bit of turbulence on an airline flight. Therefore, the job of companies operating in conditions of inherent variability is to give users what they desperately crave in conditions of low control—a sense of agency.

For instance, before Uber and its competitors arrived on the scene, catching a ride to the airport was a stressful experience. You'd have to call a taxi dispatcher, tell them where you were waiting, and ask how long it would take for the cab to pick you up. The taxi company had little idea how long it would take the driver to get to you so would always tell you, "We'll be there soon." Soon? But when? Sometimes it would take the driver fifteen minutes, sometimes twenty or forty-five, all the while leaving the passenger very uncertain and worrying about making their boarding time.

Compare this experience to requesting an Uber ride today through the company's app. Using a Pac-Man-like interface, the passenger can see exactly how far away their ride is and the estimated time of arrival. Of course, that time is often inaccurate, but that matters less than you'd think. The important thing is to give the user a sense of agency over something nobody has control over, namely, the flow of traffic.

Whether the product is an enterprise-focused service helping customers get a grip on the effectiveness of their marketing spend, a financial information portal, a health tracking app, or a corporate dashboard, all sorts of products operate in conditions of inherent variability. Companies building these sorts of products and services need not necessarily add more uncertainty, but rather give the user a greater sense of agency and control over inherently variable circumstances.

Which Rewards Should You Offer?

Fundamentally, variable reward systems must satisfy users' needs while leaving them wanting to reengage. As described, the most habit-forming products and services utilize one or more of the three variable rewards types: the tribe, the hunt, and the self. In fact, many habit-forming products offer multiple variable rewards.

E-mail, for example, utilizes all three variable reward types. What subconsciously compels us to check our e-mail? First, there is uncertainty concerning who might be sending us a message. We have a social obligation to respond to e-mails and a desire to be seen as agreeable (rewards of the tribe). We may also be curious about what information is in the e-mail: Perhaps something related to our career or business awaits us? Checking e-mail informs us of opportunities or threats to our material possessions and livelihood (rewards of the hunt). Lastly, e-mail is in itself a task—challenging us to sort, categorize, and act to eliminate unread messages. We are motivated by the uncertain nature of our fluctuating e-mail count and feel compelled to gain control of our in-box (rewards of the self).

As B. F. Skinner discovered over fifty years ago, variable rewards are a powerful inducement to repeat actions. Understanding what moves users to return to habit-forming products gives designers an opportunity to build products that align with their users' interests.

However, simply giving users what they want is not enough to create a habit-forming product. The feedback loop of the first three steps of the Hook—trigger, action, and variable reward—still misses a final critical phase. In the next chapter we will learn how getting people to invest their time, effort, data, or social equity in your product is a requirement for repeat use.

REMEMBER & SHARE

- *Variable reward* is the third phase of the Hooked Model, and there are three types of variable rewards: the tribe, the hunt, and the self.

- *Rewards of the tribe* is the search for social rewards fueled by connectedness with other people.

- *Rewards of the hunt* is the search for material resources and information.

- *Rewards of the self* is the search for intrinsic rewards of mastery, competence, and completion.

- When our autonomy is threatened, we feel constrained by our lack of choices and often rebel against doing a behavior. Psychologists refer to this as *reactance*. Maintaining a sense of user autonomy and trust is a requirement for sustained engagement.

- Experiences with finite variability become increasingly predictable with use and lose their appeal over time. Experiences that maintain user interest by sustaining variability with use exhibit infinite variability.

- Variable rewards must satisfy users' needs while leaving them wanting to reengage with the product.

DO THIS NOW

Refer to the answers you came up with in the last "Do This Now" section to complete the following exercises:

- Speak with five of your customers in an open-ended interview to identify what they find enjoyable or encouraging about using your product. Are there any moments of delight or surprise? Is there anything they find particularly satisfying about using the product?

- Review the steps your customer takes to use your product or service habitually. What outcome (reward) alleviates the user's pain? Is the reward fulfilling, yet leaves the user wanting more?

- Brainstorm three ways your product might heighten users' search for variable rewards using:

  1. rewards of the tribe—gratification from others.
  2. rewards of the hunt—material goods, money, or information.
  3. rewards of the self—mastery, completion, competency, or consistency.

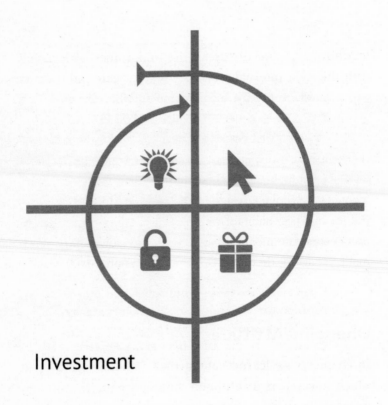

Investment

| 5 |

Investment

In chapter 2, we discussed the importance of aligning with the right internal triggers, and how external triggers can prompt users with information for the next intended action.

In chapter 3 we learned about the role of the smallest actions taken in anticipation of immediate rewards. In chapter 4 we looked at how variable outcomes influence repeat engagement. There is one last step in the Hooked Model that is critical for building habit-forming products and services. Before users create the mental associations that activate their automatic behaviors, they must first *invest* in the product.

Changing Attitude

In chapter 1 we learned about the tooth-flossing study in which researchers determined that the frequency of a new behavior is a leading factor in forming a new habit. The study also found that the second most important factor in habit formation is a change in the participant's attitude about the behavior. The finding is consistent with the Habit

Zone graph explained in the first chapter, which illustrates that for a behavior to become routine it must occur with significant frequency and perceived utility. Attitude change is the movement up the perceived utility axis until the behavior enters the Habit Zone.

But in order for a change in attitude to occur, there must be a change in how users perceive the behavior. In this chapter, we will start by exploring the mystery surrounding how small investments change our perception, turning unfamiliar actions into everyday habits.

A psychological phenomenon known as *the escalation of commitment* has been shown to make our brains do all sorts of funny things. The power of commitment makes some people play video games until they keel over and die.[1] It is used to influence people to give more to charity.[2] It has even been used to coerce prisoners of war into switching allegiances.[3] The commitments we make have a powerful effect on us and play an important role in the things we do, the products we buy, and the habits we form.

The more users invest time and effort into a product or service, the more they value it. In fact, there is ample evidence to suggest that our labor leads to love.

We Irrationally Value Our Efforts

In a 2011 study, Dan Ariely, Michael Norton, and Daniel Mochon measured the effect of labor on how people value things.[4]

U. S. college students in America were given instructions to assemble an origami crane or frog. After the exercise students were asked to purchase their creation, bidding up to $1. Assemblers were informed that a random number between zero and one hundred was to be drawn. If it exceeded their reservation price in cents, the assemblers would return empty-handed—but if it was equal to or less than their bid, they would pay their bid and keep the origami. Meanwhile, a separate group of students located in another room, unaware of the identity of the assemblers, were asked to bid on their origami using the same procedure. Similarly, a third independent group was asked to bid on expert-made origami under the same criteria.

The results showed that those who made their own origami animals valued their creation five times higher than the second group's valuation, and nearly as high as the expert-made origami values (figure 25). In other words,

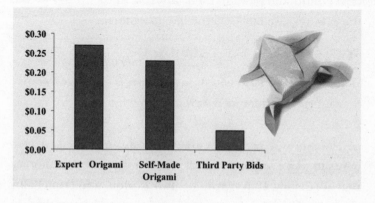

FIGURE 25

those who invested labor associated greater value with their paper creations simply because they had worked on them. Ariely calls this the IKEA effect.

IKEA, the world's largest furniture retailer, sells afford-able, ready-to-assemble household furnishings. The Swedish company's key innovation is its packaging process, which allows the company to decrease labor costs, increase distribu-tion efficiency, and better utilize the real estate in its stores.

Unlike its competitors who sell preassembled merchan-dise, IKEA puts its customers to work. It turns out there's a hidden benefit to making users invest physical effort in as-sembling the product—by asking customers to assemble their own furniture, Ariely believes they adopt an irrational love of the furniture they built, just like the test subjects did in the origami experiments. Businesses that leverage user effort confer higher value to their products simply because their users have put work into them. The users have *invested* in the products through their labor.

We Seek to Be Consistent with Our Past Behaviors

Studies reveal that our past is an excellent predictor of our future.

A team of researchers asked a group of suburban resi-dents to place large, unsightly signs in front of their homes that read DRIVE CAREFULLY.[5] Two groups were tested. In the first group only 17 percent of the subjects agreed to the request, while 76 percent of those in the second group agreed to post the ugly yard signs. What was the cause of this huge discrepancy? The groups were identical except for one factor.

Those in the second group were approached two weeks prior to the yard sign request and asked to place a much smaller, three-inch sign that read BE A SAFE DRIVER in their windows. Nearly everyone who was asked to place the smaller message agreed to this. When the researchers returned two weeks later, a whopping majority of these residents willingly replaced the small sign with the large one on their front lawns.

The homeowners' greater willingness to place the large, obtrusive sign on their lawns after agreeing to the smaller one demonstrates the impact of our predilection for consistency with our past behaviors. Little investments, such as placing a tiny sign in a window, can lead to big changes in future behaviors.

We Avoid Cognitive Dissonance

In a classic Aesop's fable, a hungry fox encounters grapes hanging from a vine. The fox desperately wants the grapes. Yet as hard as he tries, he cannot reach them. Frustrated, the fox decides the grapes must be sour and that therefore he would not want them anyway.

The fox comforts himself by changing his perception of

the grapes because it is too uncomfortable to reconcile the thought that the grapes are sweet and ready for the taking, and yet he cannot have them. To reconcile these two conflicting ideas, the fox changes his perception of the grapes and in the process relieves the pain of what psychologists term *cognitive dissonance.*

The irrational manipulation of the way one sees the world is not limited to fictional animals in children's stories. We humans do this as well.

Consider your reaction the first time you sipped a beer or tried spicy food. Was it tasty? Unlikely. Our bodies are designed to reject alcohol and capsaicin, the compound that creates the sensation of heat in spicy food. Our innate reaction to these acquired tastes is to reject them, yet we learn to like them through repeated exposure. We see others enjoying them, try a little more, and over time condition ourselves. To avoid the cognitive dissonance of not liking something that others seem to take so much pleasure in, we slowly change our perception of the thing we once did not enjoy.

Together, the three tendencies just described influence our future actions: The more effort we put into something, the more likely we are to value it; we are more likely to be consistent with our past behaviors; and finally, we change our preferences to avoid cognitive dissonance.

These tendencies of ours lead to a mental process known

as *rationalization*, in which we change our attitudes and beliefs to adapt psychologically. Rationalization helps us give
reasons for our behaviors, even when those reasons might
have been designed by others.

At a 2010 industry conference, Jesse Schell, a renowned
game designer and professor at Carnegie Mellon University, articulated the peculiar train of thought some players
exhibit online.[6] Schell examined *Mafia Wars*, one of Zynga's
first breakout hits, which, like *FarmVille*, attracted millions
of players.

"There's definitely a lot of psychology here, because if
someone had said, 'Hey, we're going to make a text-based
mafia game that's going to make over $100 million,' you'd
say, 'I don't think you'll do that.' Right?" Schell said, chan-
neling the critics of the day who originally dismissed the
free, primarily text-based online game. Yet Zynga used its
understanding of human psychology to build an irresistible
product at the time.

Mafia Wars was among the first games to utilize information about players' Facebook friends. "It's not just a virtual world anymore. It's your real friends." Schell said. "And
you're playing and it's kind of cool . . . but then, hey, hey,
my real friend is better than me. How can I remedy that?
Well, I can play a long time or I could just put twenty dollars
in—*aha*! It's even better if that twenty dollars I put in vali-
dates something I know is true, that I am greater than my
college roommate, Steve."

Schell went on, "Combine that with the psychological

idea . . . of rationalization, that anything you spend time on, you start to believe, 'This must be worthwhile. Why? Because I've spent time on it!' And therefore it must be worth me kicking in twenty dollars because look at the time I've spent on it. And now that I've kicked in twenty dollars, it must be valuable because only an idiot would kick in twenty dollars if it wasn't."

Schell's description of the quirky process of *Mafia Wars* rationalization helps demonstrate the strange logic of how we change our preferences. When players contemplate making a purchase, they acknowledge it is unwise to spend money on something that is not good. Yet just like the fox that perceives the grapes as sour to reduce his frustration at not being able to reach them, players justify their purchases to help convince themselves of something they want to be true—namely, that they are not foolish. The only solution is to keep paying to keep playing.

The cognitive changes that lead to behavior change help power the shift in how we view the products and services we use. But how are habit-forming products designed for user investment? How can a product keep users committed to a service until it becomes a habit?

BITS OF WORK

In a standard feedback loop the cue, action, and re-ward cycle can change our immediate behavior. For example, a radar-equipped sign is an effective way to make drivers immediately slow down by showing them their car's speed relative to the posted speed limit.

Yet this pattern differs when it comes to how we form habits with products. The Hooked Model is not just a framework for changing one-time behaviors; it is a design pattern to create unprompted engagement in order to connect the user's problem to the designer's product. To form the associations needed to create unprompted user engagement, something more than the three-step feedback loop is required.

The last step of the Hooked Model is the *investment phase*, the point at which users are asked to do a bit of work. Here, users are prompted to put something of value into the system, which increases the likeli-hood of their using the product and of successive passes through the cycle.

Unlike in the action phase of the Hook discussed in chapter 3, investments are about the anticipation of longer-term rewards, not immediate gratification.

In Twitter, for example, the investment comes in the form of following another user. There is no imme-diate reward for following someone, no stars or badges to affirm the action. Following is an investment in the service, which increases the likelihood of the user checking Twitter in the future.

Also in contrast to the action phase, the investment phase increases friction. This certainly breaks conventional thinking in the product design community that all user experiences should be as easy and effortless as possible. This approach still generally holds true, as does my advice in the action phase to make the intended actions as simple as possible. In the investment phase, however, asking users to do a bit of work comes *after* users have received variable rewards, not before. The timing of asking for user investment is critically important. By asking for the investment after the reward, the company has an opportunity to leverage a central trait of human behavior.

In an experiment conducted by Stanford researchers, two groups of people were asked to complete a task with the help of computers.[7] The participants were initially asked to use their assigned computers to answer a series of questions. The computers provided to the first group were helpful when answering participants' questions, while those provided to the second group were programmed to be unhelpful, offering unclear answers. After completing the task, participants then switched roles and the machines began asking the people for assistance with their questions.

The study found that the group given helpful computers performed almost twice as much work for their machines. The results showed that reciprocation is not just a characteristic expressed between people, but also a trait observed when humans interact with machines. Conceivably, we humans evolved the tendency to reciprocate kindness because it improved our species' ability to survive. As it turns out, we invest in products and services for the same reasons we put effort into our relationships.

The big idea behind the investment phase is to leverage the user's understanding that the service will get better with use (and personal investment). Like a good friendship, the more effort people put in, the more both parties benefit.

Storing Value

Unlike physical goods in the real world, the software that runs our technology products can adapt itself to our needs. To become better with use, habit-forming technology utilizes investments users make in the product to enhance the experience.

The stored value users put into the product increases the likelihood they will use it again in the future and comes in a variety of forms.

Content

Every time users of Spotify listen to music using the streaming service, they strengthen their ties to the product. Neither Spotify nor their users created the songs, yet the more users consume content, the more valuable the service becomes.

Spotify uses the small investment of songs played in order to assemble a selection of tunes users haven't previously heard but are likely to enjoy, called "Discover Weekly" (figure 26).

With continued investment, the service gets better at learning users' tastes and provides tailor-made suggestions. As
a demonstration of the loyalty that good content recommendations can engender, Spotify user Amanda Whitbred
tweeted, "At this point @Spotify's discover weekly knows me
so well that if it proposed I'd say yes."[8]

Spotify's personalized music recommendations are an
example of how technology adapts and improves based on
users' investment in content.

Content can also be created by a service's users. For example, every status update, "like," photo, or video shared

FIGURE 26

on Facebook adds to the user's timeline, retelling the story of one's past experiences and relationships. As users continue to share and interact with information on the service, their digital life is recorded and archived.

> *The collection of memories and experiences, in aggregate, becomes more valuable over time and the service becomes harder to leave as users' personal investment in the site grows.*

Data

Information generated, collected, or created by users (e.g., songs, photos, or news clippings) are examples of stored value in the form of content. Sometimes, though, users invest in a service by either actively or passively adding their own personal data.

On LinkedIn the user's online résumé embodies the concept of data as stored value. Every time job seekers use the service, they are prompted to add more information.

> *The company found that the more information users invested in the site, the more committed they became to it.*

As Josh Elman, an early senior product manager at the company, told me, "If we could get users to enter just a little information, they were much more likely to return." The tiny bit of effort associated with providing more user data created a powerful hook to bring people back to the service.

Mint.com is an online personal finance tool used by millions of Americans. The service aggregates all of the user's accounts in one place, providing a complete picture of their financial life—but only if they invest their time and data in the service. Mint provides multiple opportunities for users to customize the site and make it more valuable with use. For example, the act of linking accounts, categorizing transactions, or creating a budget are all forms of investment. The more data collected, the more the service's stored value increases (figure 27).

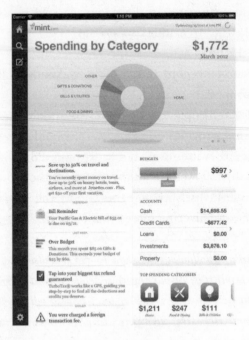

FIGURE 27

Followers

On the morning of Twitter's initial public offering on November 7, 2013, a news commentator on Bloomberg Television said that "the technology needed to build the company could be built in a day."[9] In fact, he was right. Twitter is a simple application. With a bit of basic programming know-how, anyone can build their very own clone of the multibillion-dollar social media behemoth.

In fact, several companies have tried to supplant the popular social network. One of the most notable attempts came from a disgruntled developer who decided to build App.net, an ad-free alternative that many tech industry watchers argue is actually a better product. However, like other attempts to copy the service, App.net failed to take off. Why is this?

Collecting people to follow on Twitter, as well as collecting followers, provides tremendous value and is a key driver of what keeps Twitter users hooked (figure 28).

From the follower side of the equation, the more Twitter users curate the list of people they follow, the better the service will be at delivering interesting content.

Investing in following the right people increases the value of the product by displaying more relevant and interesting content in each user's Twitter feed. It also tells Twitter a lot about its users, which in turn improves the service overall.

FIGURE 28

For the tweeter seeking followers, the more followers one has, the more valuable the service becomes as well. Content creators on Twitter seek to reach as large an audience as possible. The only way to legitimately acquire new followers is to send tweets others think are interesting enough to warrant following the sender. Therefore, to acquire more followers, content creators must invest in producing more—

and better—tweets. The cycle increases the value of the service for both sides the more the service is used. For many users, switching services means abandoning years of investment and starting over. No one wants to rebuild a loyal following they have worked hard to acquire and nurture.

Reputation

Reputation is a form of stored value users can literally take to the bank. On online marketplaces such as eBay, Upwork, Yelp, and Airbnb, people with negative scores are treated very differently from those with good reputations. It can often be the deciding factor in what price a seller gets for an item on eBay, who is selected for an Upwork job, which restaurants appear at the top of Yelp search results, and the price of a room rental on Airbnb.

On eBay both buyers and sellers take their reputations very seriously. The e-commerce giant surfaces user-generated quality scores for every buyer and seller, and awards its most active users with badges to symbolize their trustworthiness. Businesses with bad reputations find it difficult, if not impossible, to compete against highly rated sellers. Reputation is a form of stored value that increases the likelihood of using a service.

Reputation makes users, both buyers and sellers, more likely to stick with whichever service they have invested their efforts in to maintain a high-quality score (figure 29).

FIGURE 29

Skill

Investing time and effort into learning to use a product is a form of investment and stored value. Once a user has acquired a skill, using the service becomes easier and moves them to the right on the ability axis of the Fogg Behavior Model we discussed in chapter 3. As Fogg describes it, non-routine is a factor of simplicity, and the more familiar a behavior is, the more likely the user is to do it.

For example, Adobe Photoshop is the most widely used professional graphics editing program in the world. The software provides hundreds of advanced features for creating and manipulating images. Learning the program is difficult at first, but as users become more familiar with the product—often investing hours watching tutorials and reading how-to guides—their expertise and efficiency using the product improves. They also achieve a sense of mastery (rewards of the self, as discussed in chapter 4). Unfortunately for the design professional, most of this acquired knowledge by users does not translate to competing applications.

> *Once users have invested the effort to acquire a skill, they are less likely to switch to a competing product.*

Like every phase in the Hooked Model, the investment phase requires careful use. It is not a *carte blanche* tool for asking users to do onerous tasks. In fact, quite the opposite. Just as in the action phase described in chapter 3, to achieve the intended behavior in the investment phase, the product designer must consider whether users have sufficient motivation and ability to engage in the intended behavior. If users are not doing what the designer intended in the investment phase, the designer may be asking them to do too much. I recommend that you progressively stage the investment you want from users into small chunks of work, starting with small, easy tasks and building up to harder tasks during successive cycles through the Hooked Model.

As we have just seen, users store value in the service during the investment phase. However, one other key opportunity found in the investment phase greatly increases the likelihood of users returning.

Loading the Next Trigger

As described in chapter 2, triggers bring users back to the product. Ultimately, habit-forming products create a mental association with an internal trigger. Yet to create the habit, users must first use the product through multiple cycles of the Hooked Model. Therefore, external triggers must be used to bring users back around again to start another cycle.

> *Habit-forming technologies leverage the user's past behavior to initiate an external trigger in the future.*

Users set future triggers during the investment phase, providing companies with an opportunity to reengage the user. We will now explore a few examples of how companies have helped load the next trigger during the investment phase.

1. Any.do

User retention is a challenge for any business, but especially for consumer mobile applications. According to a study by a mobile analytics firm, 26 percent of mobile apps were downloaded and used only once.[10] Further data suggests people are using more applications but engaging with them less frequently.[11]

Any.do is a simple mobile task-management app used to record to-do items such as picking up dry cleaning, restocking the fridge with milk, or calling Mom. Recognizing the challenge of retaining fickle mobile consumers, the app is designed to direct users to invest early on. During the first use of the app, Any.do elegantly teaches how to use the product (figure 30). The trigger comes in the form of the app's clear, easy-to-follow instructions. The follow-up action is doing what the app tells the user to do. The variable rewards arrive in the

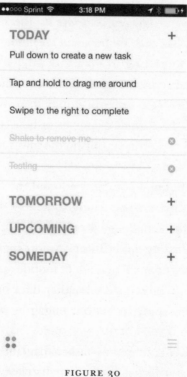

FIGURE 30

form of a congratulatory message and the satisfaction of mastering the app.

The investment comes next. Newcomers are instructed to connect the app to their calendar service, granting Any.do access to the user's schedule. In doing so, users give the app permission to send a notification after the next scheduled meeting ends. This external trigger prompts users to return to the app to record a follow-up task from the meeting they just attended. In the Any.do scenario the app sends an external trigger to users at the moment when they are most likely to experience the internal trigger of anxiety about forgetting to do a task after a meeting. The Any.do app has anticipated a need and sets users up for success.

2. Tinder

In mid-2013 a hot new company entered the hypercompetitive online dating market. Tinder quickly captured the attention of millions of people looking for love with a simple interface, generating 3.5 million matches from 350 million swipes each day.[12]

After launching the mobile app, users browse profiles of other singles. Each potential match is presented as a card. Swipe left if you are not interested, right if that special someone catches your fancy (figure 31). If both parties express interest, a match is made and a private chat connects the two potential lovebirds.

FIGURE 31

By simplifying the investment of sorting through potential mates, Tinder makes loading the next trigger more
likely with each swipe. The more swipes, the more potential
matches are made; naturally, each match sends notifications to both interested parties.

3. Snapchat

As of June 2013, Snapchat, the popular photo-sharing app, boasted of 5 million daily active users collectively sending over 200 million photos and videos daily.[13] This tremendous engagement means an average Snapchat user sends forty photos every day!

Why are users so in love with Snapchat? Its success can largely be attributed to the fact that users load the next trigger every time they use the service. Snapchat is more than a way to share images. It is a means of communication akin to sending a text message—with the added bonus of a built-in timer that can, based on the sender's instructions, cause the message to self-destruct after viewing. Users pass through the investment phase of the Hooked Model each time they send a selfie, doodle, or goofy photo. Each photo or video sent contains an implicit prompt to respond; the Snapchat interface makes returning a pic incredibly easy by twice tapping the original message to reply. The self-destruct feature encourages timely responses, leading to a back-and-forth relay that keeps people hooked into the service by loading the next trigger with each message sent.

4. Pinterest

Like many social networks, Pinterest loads the next trigger during the investment phase of the Hook. For many of the site's 250 million monthly users, the online pin board replaced the habit of browsing fashion-focused Web sites—and before the web, flipping through magazines and dog-earing favorite pages.[14]

The internal trigger for users is often boredom, for which the site offers a quick cure. Once registered, the only action required of users is to start scrolling as Pinterest showcases a wealth of variable rewards. First, because Pinterest is a socially curated collection of interesting items, the site displays a powerful intermittent reward surrounding the hunt for objects of desire, even if they are only images. The site also provides a means of communicating with friends and people who share similar tastes. The rewards of the tribe come from the variability of posting images as a communication medium. A user might be curious to know what a friend has pinned not only because of the image itself, but because of her relationship with the pinner.

Finally, Pinterest users invest in the site every time they pin an image of their own, repin someone else's image, comment on, or like a piece of content on the site (figure 32). Each of these tiny investments gives Pinterest data it can use to tailor the site to each user's individual taste; it also loads the next trigger. Each pin, repin, like, or comment gives Pinterest tacit permission to contact the user with a notification when someone else contributes to the thread, triggering the desire to visit the site again to learn more.

FIGURE 32

Pinterest clearly demonstrates the four stages of the Hooked Model. It is a seamless flow: from the itch of the internal trigger that moves users to the intended action, through the variable reward, and finally to the investment, which also loads the next external trigger. Pinterest users move through the Hook cycle from beginning to end, then happily return to the starting point for another go-round.

In this chapter we have learned how an investment in the product serves as the string that pulls the user back. To do this, the habit-forming technology increases the value of the product with each pass through the Hook. Through successive cycles of the Hooked Model, users increase their affinity for the experience. They increasingly come to rely on the product as the solution to their problems until finally, the new habit—and routine—is formed.

The more users invest in a product through tiny bits of work, the more valuable the product becomes in their lives. Users do not stay hooked forever, though. Invariably, the next big thing will come along and provide a better, more compelling hook. However, by creating habits fueled by investments in a product or service, companies make switching to a competitor difficult. User habits are hard to break and confer powerful competitive advantages to any company fortunate enough to successfully create them.

REMEMBER & SHARE

- The *investment phase* is the fourth step in the Hooked Model.

  - Unlike the action phase, which delivers immediate gratification, the investment phase concerns the anticipation of rewards in the future.

- Investments in a product create preferences because of our tendency to overvalue our work, be consistent with past behaviors, and avoid cognitive dissonance.

- Investment comes after the variable reward phase, when users are primed to reciprocate.

- Investments increase the likelihood of users returning by improving the service the more it is used. They enable the accrual of stored value in the form of content, data, followers, reputation, or skill.

- Investments increase the likelihood of users passing through the Hook again by loading the next trigger to start the cycle all over again.

DO THIS NOW

Refer to the answers you came up with in the last "Do This Now" section to complete the following exercises:

- Review your flow. What "bit of work" are your users doing to increase their likelihood of returning?

- Brainstorm three ways to add small investments into your product to:

  - Load the next trigger.

  - Store value as data, content, followers, reputation, and skill.

- Identify how long it takes for a "loaded trigger" to reengage your users. How can you reduce the delay to shorten time spent cycling through the Hook?

| 6 |

What Are You Going to Do with This?

The Hooked Model is designed to connect the user's problem with the designer's solution frequently enough to form a habit. It is a framework for building products that solve user needs through long-term engagement.

As users pass through cycles of the Hooked Model, they learn to meet their needs with the habit-forming product. Effective hooks transition users from relying upon external triggers to cueing mental associations with internal triggers. Users move from states of low engagement to high engagement, from low preference to high preference.

You are now equipped to use the Hooked Model to ask yourself these fundamental questions for building effective hooks:

1. What do users really want? What pain is your product relieving? (*Internal trigger*)
2. What brings users to your service? (*External trigger*)
3. What is the simplest action users take in anticipation of reward, and how can you simplify your product to make this action easier? (*Action*)

4. Are users fulfilled by the reward yet left wanting more? (*Variable reward*)
5. What "bit of work" do users invest in your product? Does it load the next trigger and store value to improve the product with use? (*Investment*)

The Morality of Manipulation

Now that you're aware of the pattern for building habit-forming technology, how will you use this knowledge?

Perhaps while reading this book you asked yourself if the Hooked Model is a recipe for manipulation. Maybe you felt a bit unsettled reading what seemed like a cookbook for mind control. If so, that is a very good thing.

The Hooked Model is fundamentally about changing people's behaviors, but the power to build persuasive products should be used with caution.

Creating habits can be a force for good, but it can also be used for nefarious purposes. What responsibility do product makers have when creating user habits?

Let's admit it: We are all in the persuasion business.[1] Innovators build products meant to persuade people to do what we want them to do. We call these people *users* and even if we don't say it aloud, we secretly wish every one of them would become fiendishly hooked to whatever we're making. I'm guessing that's likely why you started reading this book.

Users take their technologies with them to bed.[2] When they wake up, they check for notifications, tweets, and updates, sometimes even before saying "Good morning" to their loved ones. Ian Bogost, the famed game creator and professor, calls the wave of habit-forming technologies the "cigarette of this century" and warns of their equally addictive and potentially destructive side effects.[3]

You may be asking, "When is it wrong to manipulate users?"

Manipulation is an experience crafted to change behavior—we all know what it feels like. We're uncomfortable when we sense someone is trying to make us do something we wouldn't do otherwise, like when sitting through a car salesman's spiel or hearing a time-share presentation.

Yet manipulation doesn't always have a negative connotation. If manipulation is an experience crafted to change behavior, then Weight Watchers, one of the most successful mass-manipulation products in history, fits the definition.[4] Weight Watchers customers' decisions are programmed by the designer of the system, yet few question the morality of the business.

What, therefore, is the difference? Why is manipulating users through flashy advertising or an engaging video game thought to be distasteful while a strict system of food rationing is considered laudable? Although many people see

Weight Watchers as an acceptable form of user manipulation, our moral compass has not caught up with what the latest technology now makes possible.

Ubiquitous access to the web, transferring greater amounts of personal data at faster speeds than ever before, has created a more potentially addictive world. According to famed Silicon Valley investor Paul Graham, we haven't had time to develop societal "antibodies to addictive new things."[5] Graham places responsibility on the user: "Unless we want to be canaries in the coal mine of each new addiction—the people whose sad example becomes a lesson to future generations—we'll have to figure out for ourselves what to avoid and how."

What of the people, then, who make these manipulative experiences? After all, the corporations that unleash these habit-forming, at times downright addictive technologies are made up of human beings with a moral sense of right and wrong. They too have families and kids who are susceptible to manipulation. What shared responsibilities do we so-called growth hackers and behavior designers have to our users, to future generations, and to ourselves?

With the increasing pervasiveness and persuasiveness of personal technology, some industry insiders have proposed creating an ethical code of conduct.[6] Others believe differently: Chris Nodder, author of the book *Evil by Design*, writes, "It's OK to deceive people if it's in their best interests, or if they've given implicit consent to be deceived as part of a persuasive strategy."[7]

I offer the Manipulation Matrix, a simple decision-support tool entrepreneurs, employees, and investors can use long before product is shipped or code is written. The Manipulation Matrix does not try to answer which businesses are moral or which will succeed, nor does it describe what can and cannot become a habit-forming technology. The matrix seeks to help you answer not "Can I hook my users?" but instead "Should I attempt to?"

To use the Manipulation Matrix (figure 33), the maker needs to ask two questions. First, "Would I use the product myself?" and second, "Will the product help users materially improve their lives?"

Remember, this framework is for creating habit-forming products, not one-time-use goods. Let's explore the types of creators who represent the four quadrants of the Manipulation Matrix.

Manipulation Matrix

	The maker does not use it	The maker uses it
Materially improves the user's life	Peddler	Facilitator
Does not improve the user's life	Dealer	Entertainer

FIGURE 33

1. The Facilitator

When you create something that you would use, that you believe makes the user's life better, you are facilitating a healthy habit. It is important to note that only you can decide if you would actually use the product or service, and what "materially improving the life of the user" really means in light of what you are creating.

If you find yourself squirming as you ask yourself these questions or needing to qualify or justify your answers, *stop!* You failed. You have to truly want to use the product and believe it materially benefits your life as well as the lives of your users.

One exception is if you would have been a user in your younger years. For example, in the case of an education company, you may not need to use the service right now but are certain you would have used it in your not-so-distant past. Note, however, that the further you are from your former self, the lower your odds of success.

In building a habit for a user other than you, you cannot consider yourself a facilitator unless you have experienced the problem firsthand.

Jake Harriman grew up on a small farm in West Virginia. After graduating from the United States Naval Academy, Harriman served as an infantry and special operations platoon commander in the Marine Corps. He was in Iraq during the 2003 invasion and led men into fierce gun battles with enemy combatants. He assisted with disaster relief in Indonesia and Sri Lanka after the 2004 Asian tsunami.

Harriman maintains that his encounter with extreme poverty abroad changed his life. After seven and a half years of active duty, Harriman realized that guns alone could not stop terrorists intent on harming Americans. "Desperate people commit desperate acts," Harriman says. After his service Harriman founded Nuru International, a social venture targeting extreme poverty by changing the habits of people living in rural areas.

However, exactly how Harriman would change the lives of the poorest people in the world was not clear to him until he decided to live among them. In Kenya he discovered that basic practices of modern agriculture, like proper seed spacing, were still not used. Yet Harriman knew that simply teaching farmers new behaviors would not be enough.

Instead, by drawing upon his own rural upbringing and experience living with the farmers, Harriman uncovered the obstacles in their way. He soon learned that the lack of access to financing for high-quality seeds and fertilizer kept farmers from utilizing yield-boosting techniques.

Nuru is currently equipping farmers in Kenya and Ethiopia, helping them rise out of grinding poverty. It was only by becoming one of his users that Harriman could design solutions to meet their needs.[8]

Although it is a long way from Africa to Silicon Valley, the well-documented stories of the founders of Facebook, Slack, Google, and Twitter reveal they would likely see themselves as making products in the facilitator quadrant. A new breed of companies is now creating products to improve lives by implementing healthy habits. Whether getting users to exercise more, save money, or be more productive at work, these companies are run by authentic entrepreneurs who desperately want their products to exist, products that stem from a desire to satisfy their own needs.

However, what if the usage of a well-intended product becomes extreme, even harmful? What about the users who go beyond forming habits and become full-fledged addicts?

First, it is important to recognize that the percentage of users who form a detrimental dependency is very small. Industry estimates for pathological users of even the most habit-forming technologies, such as slot-machine gambling, are just 1 percent.[9] Addiction tends to manifest in people with a particular psychological profile. However, simply brushing off the issue as too small to matter dismisses the very real problems caused by technology addiction.

For the first time though, companies have access to data that could be used to flag which users are using their products too much. Whether companies choose to act on that data in a way that aids their users is naturally a question of corporate responsibility. Companies building habit-forming technologies have a moral obligation—and perhaps someday a legal mandate—to inform and protect users who are forming unhealthy attachments to their products. It would behoove entrepreneurs building potentially addictive products to set guidelines for identifying and helping addicted users.

Yet for the overwhelming majority of users, addiction to a product will never be a problem.

> *Even though the world is becoming a potentially more addictive place, most people have the ability to self-regulate their behaviors.*

The role of facilitator fulfills the moral obligation for entrepreneurs building a product they will themselves use and that they believe materially improves the lives of others. As long as they have procedures in place to assist those who form unhealthy addictions, the designer can act with a clean conscience. To take liberties with Mahatma Gandhi's famous quote, facilitators "*build* the change they want to see in the world."

2. The Peddler

Heady altruistic ambitions can at times outpace reality. Too often, designers of manipulative technology have a strong motivation to improve the lives of their users, but when pressed they admit they would not actually use their own creations. Their holier-than-thou products often try to "gamify" some task no one really wants to do by inserting run-of-the-mill incentives such as badges or points that don't actually hold value for their users.

Fitness apps, charity Web sites, and products that claim to suddenly turn hard work into fun often fall into this quadrant. Possibly the most common example of peddlers, though, is in advertising.

Countless companies convince themselves they're making ad campaigns users will love. They expect their videos to go viral and their branded apps to be used daily. Their so-called reality distortion fields keep them from asking the critical question, "Would I actually find this useful?"[10] The answer to this uncomfortable question is nearly always no, so they twist their thinking until they can imagine a user they believe might find the ad valuable.

Materially improving users' lives is a tall order, and attempting to create a persuasive technology that you do not use yourself is incredibly difficult. This puts designers at a heavy disadvantage because of their disconnect with their products and users. There's nothing immoral about peddling; in fact, many companies working on solutions for others do so out of purely altruistic reasons. It's just that the odds of successfully designing products for a customer you don't know extremely well are depressingly low.

Peddlers tend to lack the empathy and insights needed to create something users truly want.

Often the peddler's project results in a time-wasting failure because the designers did not fully understand their users. As a result, no one finds the product useful.

3. The Entertainer

Sometimes makers of products just want to have fun. If creators of a potentially addictive technology make something that they use but can't in good conscience claim improves users' lives, they're making entertainment.

Entertainment is art and is important for its own sake. Art provides joy, helps us see the world differently, and connects us with the human condition. These are all important and age-old pursuits. Entertainment, however, has particular attributes of which the entrepreneur, employee, and investor should be aware when using the Manipulation Matrix.

Art is often fleeting; products that form habits around entertainment tend to fade quickly from users' lives. A hit song, repeated over and over again in the mind, becomes nostalgia after it is replaced by the next chart-topper. A book like this one is read and thought about for a while until the next interesting piece of brain candy comes along. As we learned in the chapter on variable rewards, games like *Farm-Ville* and *Angry Birds* engross users, but are then relegated to the gaming dustbin along with other hyper-engaging has-beens such as *Pac-Man* and *Mario Bros.*

Entertainment is a hits-driven business because the

brain reacts to stimulus by wanting more and more of it, ever hungry for continuous novelty.

Building an enterprise on ephemeral desires is akin to running on an incessantly rolling treadmill: You have to keep up with the constantly changing demands of your users.

In this quadrant the sustainable business is not purely the game, the song, or the book—profit comes from an effective distribution system for getting those goods to market while they're still hot, and at the same time keeping the pipeline full of fresh releases to feed an eager audience.

4. The Dealer

Creating a product that the designer does not believe improves users' lives and that he himself would not use is called exploitation.

In the absence of these two criteria, presumably the only reason the designer is hooking users is to make a buck. Certainly, there is money to be made getting users to do things that do little more than extract cash; and where there is cash, there will be someone willing to take it.

The question is: Is that someone you? Casinos and drug dealers offer users a good time, but when the action harms the user, the fun stops.

In a satirical take on Zynga's *FarmVille* franchise, Ian Bogost created *Cow Clicker*, a Facebook game in which users did nothing but incessantly click on virtual cows to hear a satisfying *moo*.[11] Bogost intended to lampoon *FarmVille* by blatantly implementing the same game mechanics and viral hacks he thought would be laughably obvious to users. But after the app's usage exploded and some people became frighteningly obsessed with the game, Bogost shut it down, bringing on what he called the "Cowpocalypse."[12]

Bogost rightfully compared addictive technology to cigarettes. Certainly, the incessant need for a smoke in what was once a majority of the adult U.S. population has been replaced by a nearly equal compulsion to constantly check our electronic devices. Yet unlike the addiction to nicotine, new technologies offer an opportunity to dramatically improve users' lives. Like all technologies, recent advances in the habit-forming potential of digital innovation have both positive and negative effects.

If the innovator has a clear conscience that the product materially improves people's lives—first among them, the designer's—then the only path is to push forward. With the exception of the addicted 1 percent and other protected classes like children, users bear ultimate responsibility for their actions.

However, as the march of technology makes the world a potentially more addictive place, innovators need to consider their role. It will be years, perhaps generations, before society develops the social antibodies to control new

habits; in the meantime many of these behaviors may develop harmful side effects. For now, users must learn to assess these yet-unknown consequences for themselves, while
creators will have to live with the moral repercussions of
how they spend their professional lives.

My hope is that the Manipulation Matrix helps innovators consider the implications of the products they create.
Perhaps after reading this book, you'll start a new business.
Maybe you'll join an existing company with a mission to
which you are committed. Possibly, you will decide it is time
to quit your job because you've come to realize it no longer
points in the same direction as your moral compass.

REMEMBER & SHARE

- To help you, as a designer of habit-forming technology, assess the morality behind how you manipulate users, it is helpful to determine which of
  the four categories your work fits into. Are you a
  facilitator, peddler, entertainer, or dealer?

- *Facilitators* use their own product and believe
  it can materially improve people's lives. They
  have the highest chance of success because
  they most closely understand the needs of
  their users.

- *Peddlers* believe their product can materially improve people's lives but do not use it themselves.

They must beware of the hubris and inauthenticity that comes from building solutions for people they do not understand firsthand.

- *Entertainers* use their product but do not believe it can improve people's lives. They can be successful, but without making the lives of others better in some way, the entertainer's products often lack staying power.

- *Dealers* neither use the product nor believe it can improve people's lives. They have the lowest chance of finding long-term success and often find themselves in morally precarious positions.

DO THIS NOW

- Take a minute to consider where you fall on the Manipulation Matrix. Do you use your own product or service? Does it influence positive or negative behaviors? How does it make you feel? Ask yourself if you are proud of the way you are influencing the behavior of others.

| 7 |

Case Studies

THE BIBLE APP

In the previous chapter I urged you to be a facilitator and use the tools in this book to improve the lives of others. I encouraged you to align your work with a purpose that provides you with meaning and helps cultivate meaning for others. This is not only a moral imperative, it's good business practice.

> *The most highly regarded entrepreneurs are driven by meaning, a vision for greater good that drives them forward.*

Start-ups are grueling and only the most fortunate persevere before finding success. If you only build for fame or fortune, you will likely find neither. Build for meaning, though, and you can't go wrong.

The Hooked Model is a framework based on human psychology and a close examination of today's most successful habit-forming products. Now that you have an understanding of the model and the psychology behind why we do the things we do, let's study how it all comes together in one of the world's most popular apps. Whether or not you agree with the mission of the app described below is unimportant. The lesson here is how a technology company created a user habit while staying true to the founder's moral calling.

It's not often an app has the power to keep someone out of a strip club. Yet according to Bobby Gruenewald, CEO of YouVersion, that's exactly what his technology did. Gruenewald says a user of his Bible verse app walked into a business of ill repute when suddenly, seemingly out of the heavens, he received a notification on his phone. "God's trying to tell me something!" Gruenewald recalled the user saying. "I just walked into a strip club—and, man—the Bible just texted me!"

In July 2013 YouVersion announced a monumental milestone for the app, placing it in a rare strata of technology companies. The simply named Bible App has been downloaded to more than 100 million devices and growing.[1] Gruenewald says a new install occurs every 1.3 seconds.

On average, sixty-six thousand people open the app every second—and sometimes the open rate is much higher. Every Sunday, Gruenewald says, preachers around the world tell congregants to "take out your Bibles or YouVersion app. And, we see a huge spike."

The market for religious apps is fiercely competitive. A *Bible* word search in the Apple App Store returns 5,185 results. But among all the choices, YouVersion's Bible App seems to be the chosen one, ranking at the top of the list and boasting over 641,000 reviews.

How did YouVersion come to dominate the digital

"word of God"? It turns out there is much more behind the app's success than missionary zeal. It's a case study of how technology can change behavior by marrying the principles of consumer psychology with the latest in big data analytics.

According to industry insiders, the YouVersion Bible could be worth a bundle. Jules Maltz, who is the general partner at Institutional Venture Partners (IVP), told me, "As a rule of thumb, a company this size could be worth two hundred million dollars and up."

Maltz should know. His firm announced an investment in another pre-revenue app, Snapchat, at an $800 million valuation in July 2013.[2] Maltz justifies the price by pointing to the per-user valuations of other tech companies such as Facebook, Instagram, and Twitter, each of which commanded astronomical investment sums well before turning a profit. Maltz was quick to add, "Of course, this assumes the company can monetize through advertising."

In the Beginning

Gruenewald is a quick-thinking, fast-talking man. During our conversation he pulled up statistics in real time, stopping himself midsentence whenever relevant data flashed on his screen. As Gruenewald preaches on about best practices in mobile app development, I need to occasionally interrupt him to ask clarifying questions. My words stumble over his enthusiasm as he bears witness to what he's learned building his app. He spouts user retention figures with the same gusto I'd imagine he might proclaim scripture.

"Unlike other companies, when we started, we were not building a Bible reader for seminary students. YouVersion was designed to be used by everyone, every day," Gruenewald says, attributing much of the app's success to a relentless focus on creating habitual Bible readers. The Bible App's success is broken down into the language of habit formation more commonly seen in psychology textbooks. The cues, behaviors, and rewards of communing with the Lord are bullet-pointed, ready for our discussion.

"Bible study guides are nothing new," Gruenewald says. "People have been using them with pen and paper long before we came along." But I soon find out, the Bible App is much more than a mobile study guide.

The first version of YouVersion, in fact, was not mobile at all. "We originally started as a desktop Web site, but that really didn't engage people in the Bible," explains Gruenewald. "It wasn't until we tried a mobile version that we noticed a difference in people, including ourselves, turning to the Bible more because it was on a device they always had with them."

This is not surprising. The Fogg Behavior Model (see chapter 3) notes that for an action to occur, users must receive a trigger and have sufficient motivation and ability to complete it. If any of these elements are missing or inadequate at the moment the trigger arises, the action will not occur.

The omnipresence of Bible App makes it far more accessible than its Web site predecessor, giving users the ability to open the mobile app when triggered by the pastor's instructions or when feeling inspired at other moments throughout their day. Its users take it everywhere, reading the scripture in even the most unsanctified places. The company revealed that 18 percent of readers report using the Bible App in the bathroom.[3]

How to Form a God Habit

Gruenewald acknowledges his Bible App enjoyed the good fortune of being among the first of its kind at the genesis of Apple's App Store in 2008. To take advantage of this newly established marketplace, Gruenewald quickly converted his Web site into a mobile app optimized for reading. The app caught the rising tide, but soon a wave of competition followed. If his app was to reign supreme, Gruenewald needed to get users hooked quickly.

That's when Gruenewald says he implemented a plan—actually, many plans. A signature of the Bible App is its selection of over four hundred reading plans—a devotional iTunes of sorts, catering to an audience with diverse tastes, troubles, and tongues. Given my personal interest and research into habit-forming technology, I decided to start a Bible-reading plan of my own. A plan titled "Addictions" seemed appropriate.

For those who have yet to form a routine around biblical study, reading plans provide structure and guidance. "Certain sections of the Bible can be difficult for people to get through," Gruenewald admits. "By offering reading plans with different small sections of the Bible each day, it helps keep [readers] from giving up."

The app chunks out and sequences the text by separating it into bite-size pieces.

By parsing readings into digestible communion wafer–size portions, the app focuses the reader's brain on the small task at hand while avoiding the intimidation of reading the entire book.

Holy Triggers

Five years of testing and tinkering have helped Gruenewald's team discover what works best. The Bible App's reading plans are now tuned to immaculate perfection, and Gruenewald has learned that frequency of use is paramount: "We've always focused on daily reading. Our entire structure for plans focuses on daily engagement."

To get users to open the app every day, Gruenewald makes sure he sends effective cues—like the notification sent to the sinner in the strip club. Gruenewald admits, though, that he stumbled upon the power of good triggers. "At first we were very worried about sending people notifications. We didn't want to bother them too much."

To test how much of a cyber cross users were willing to bear, Gruenewald decided to run an experiment. "For Christmas, we sent people a message from the app. Just a 'Merry Christmas' in various languages." The team was prepared to hear from disgruntled users annoyed by the message. "We were afraid people would uninstall the app," Gruenewald says. "But just the opposite happened. People took pictures of the notification on their phones and started sharing them on Instagram, Twitter, and Facebook. They felt God was reaching out to them." Today, Gruenewald says, triggers play an important role in every reading plan.

On my own plan, I receive a daily notification—an owned external trigger—on my phone. It simply says, "Don't forget to read your Addictions reading plan." Ironically, the addiction I'm trying to cure is my dependency on digital gadgetry, but what the hell, I'll fall off the wagon just this once.

In case I somehow avoid the first message, a red badge over a tiny Holy Bible icon on my phone cues me again. If I forget to start the first day of a plan, I'll receive a message suggesting that perhaps I should try a different, less-challenging plan. I also have the option of receiving verse through e-mail. And if I slip up and miss a few days, another e-mail reminds me to get back on track.

The Bible app also comes with a virtual congregation of

sorts. Members of the site tend to send encouraging words to one another, delivering even more triggers. According to the company's publicist, "Community e-mails can serve as a nudge to open the app." These relationship-based external triggers are everywhere in the Bible app and are one of the keys to keeping users engaged.

Glory Be in the Data

Gruenewald's team sifts through behavioral data collected from millions of readers to better understand what users want from the app. "We just have so much data flowing through our system," Gruenewald says. The data reveals important insights on what drives user retention. High on the list of findings is the importance of ease of use, which came up throughout our conversation.

In line with the work of psychologists from early Gestalt psychologist Kurt Lewin to modern-day researchers, the app uses the principle that by making an intended action easier to do, people will do it more often.

The Bible App is designed to make absorbing the Word as frictionless as possible. For example, to make the Bible App habit easier to adopt, users who prefer listening over reading can simply tap a small icon to play an audio track read with the dramatic bravado of Charlton Heston himself.

Gruenewald says his data also revealed that changing the order of the Bible by placing the more interesting sections up front and saving the boring bits for later increased completion rates. Furthermore, daily reading plans are kept to a simple inspirational thought and a few short verses for newcomers. The idea is to get neophytes into the ritual for a few minutes each day until the routine becomes a facet of their everyday lives.

Rewards from the Lord

Gruenewald says the connection people have with scripture taps into deep emotions that "we need to use responsibly." Readers who form a habit of using the app turn to it not only when they see a notification on their phone, but also whenever they feel low and need a way to lift their spirits.

"We believe that the Bible is a way God speaks to us," Gruenewald says. "When people see a verse, they see wisdom or truth they can apply to their lives or a situation they're going through." Skeptics might call this subjective validation, and psychologists term it *the Forer effect*, but to the faithful it amounts to personally communicating with God.

Upon opening the Bible App, I find a specially selected verse waiting for me on the topic of "Addictions." With just two taps I'm reading 1 Thessalonians 5:11—encouragement for the "children of the day," imploring them with the words, "let us be sober." It's easy to see how these comforting words could serve as a sort of prize wrapped inside the app, helping readers feel better.

Gruenewald says his Bible App also offers an element of mystery and variability. "One woman would stay up until just past midnight to know what verse she had received for her next day," Gruenewald says. The unknown—in this case, which verse will be chosen for the reader and how it relates to their personal struggle—becomes an important driver of the reading habit.

As for my own reward, after finishing my verse, I received affirmation from a satisfying "Day Complete!" screen. A check mark appeared near the scripture I had read and another one was placed on my reading plan calendar. Skipping a day would mean breaking the chain of checked days, employing the endowed progress effect (previously discussed in chapter 3)—a tactic also used by video game designers to encourage progression.

As habit forming as the Bible App's reading plans can be, they are not for everyone. In fact, Gruenewald reports most users downloaded the app but never register for an account with YouVersion. Millions choose to not follow any plan, opting instead to use the app as a substitute for their paper Bibles. But to Gruenewald, using the app in this way suits him fine. Unregistered readers are still helping to grow the app. In fact, social media is abuzz with the two hundred thousand pieces of content shared from the app every twenty-four hours.

To help spread the app, a new verse greets the reader on the first page. Below the verse a large blue button reads

"Share Verse of the Day." One click and the daily scripture is blasted to Facebook or Twitter.

The drivers behind recently read scripture have not been widely studied. However, one reason may be the reward of portraying oneself in a positive light, also known as the *humblebrag*.[4] A Harvard meta-analysis, "Disclosing information about the self is intrinsically rewarding," found the act "engages neural and cognitive mechanisms associated with reward."[5] In fact, sharing feels so good that one study found "individuals were willing to forgo money to disclose about the self."

There are many opportunities to share verse from within the Bible App, but one of Gruenewald's most effective distribution channels is not online but in row—that is, the pews where churchgoers sit side by side every week.

"People tell each other about the app because they use it surrounded by people who ask about it," Gruenewald says. The app always sees a spike in new downloads on Sundays when people are most likely to share it through word of mouth.

However, nothing signals the reign of Gruenewald's Bible App quite like the way some preachers have come to depend upon it. YouVersion lets religious leaders input their sermons into the app so their congregants can follow along in real time—book, verse, and passage—all without flipping a page. Once the head of the church is hooked, the congregation is sure to follow.

Using the Bible App at church not only has the benefit

of driving growth, it also builds commitment. Every time users highlight a verse, add a comment, create a bookmark, or share from the app, they invest in it.

As described in chapter 5, Dan Ariely and Michael Norton have shown the effect small amounts of work have on the way people value various products. This so-called IKEA effect illustrates the connection between labor and perceived worth.

It is reasonable to think that the more readers put into the Bible App in the form of small investments, the more it becomes a repository of their history of worship. Like a book that is dog-eared and filled with scribbled insights and wisdom, the app becomes a treasured asset that won't easily be discarded. The more readers use the Bible App, the more valuable it becomes to them. Switching to a different digital Bible—God forbid—becomes less likely with each new revelation users type into (or extract from) the app, further securing YouVersion's dominion.

Gruenewald claims he is not in competition with anyone, but he does on occasion rattle off app store categories where his Bible App holds a high ranking. His app's place at the top of the charts appears secure now that the Bible has crossed its hundred millionth install. Yet Gruenewald plans to continue sifting through the terabytes of data in search of new ways to increase the reach of his app and make his version of the Bible even more habit-forming. To its tens of millions of regular users, Gruenewald's app is a Godsend.

REMEMBER & SHARE

- The Bible App was far less engaging as a desktop Web site; the mobile interface increased accessibility and usage by providing frequent triggers.

- The Bible App increases users' ability to take action by front-loading interesting content and providing an alternative audio version.

- By separating the verses into small chunks, users find the Bible easier to read on a daily basis; not knowing what the next verse will be adds a variable reward.

- Every annotation, bookmark, and highlight stores data (and value) in the app, further committing users.

FITBOD

Could there be a behavior more antithetical to human nature than exercise? Our caveman ancestors, if they could observe our workout habits today, would think we've lost our minds. We lift heavy objects into the air and return them to the exact spot where we picked them up. We buy ridiculous gadgetry to get in shape (Shake Weight, anyone?). We elevate our heart rates as if we're being chased by a hungry predator. And for what? Not to escape danger, but to undo the negative consequences of our overindulgent and underactive modern lifestyles.

Americans spend $19 billion annually on gym memberships.[6] Unfortunately, while many people join gyms, few use them for long. According to the Fitness Industry Association, about 44 percent of people who sign up for a gym membership quit after just six months.[7]

While disheartening, the figure is not surprising. Humans are hardwired to value short-term rewards over long-term benefits.[8] We often choose to stay under warm bedcovers rather than invest in the future benefits of working out.

I know that dichotomy all too well. I've struggled with working out for as long as I can remember. As an obese child, my mother dragged me to the gym to help me slim down. As a lethargic teenager, I joined the high school wrestling team in a desperate attempt to get in shape, but I never won a single match. As an adult, I tried to prioritize the gym as part of my regular routine countless times but failed at each attempt.

Until I found Fitbod.

Fitbod is a beautifully designed app that has helped me consistently hit the gym for over two years, and I'm not the only one who's found the app helpful. Over three million people have downloaded Fitbod, and it's consistently ranked among the top-grossing and top-rated apps in its Apple App Store category. While the app has been incredibly useful to me, I was pleasantly surprised to learn that this book, *Hooked*, was useful to the app's founders.

Fitbod is the brainchild of Allen Chen, a fitness enthusiast who, despite lifting weights for over a decade, still had a frequent problem. "I'd walk into the gym and every single day not know what to do," he told me. "I wanted my phone to just tell me which muscles I needed to engage."

In 2015 Chen says he read *Hooked* and designed an initial prototype based on the four parts of the Hooked Model. He started with the internal trigger, the actuator of the behavior, which he identified as the uncertainty of not knowing what to do in the gym.

Once Chen had a working prototype, he shared it with his college friend, Jesse Venticinque, who was working as a designer at LinkedIn at the time. "I read *Hooked* when it made the rounds in the office," Venticinque told me. Seeing the potential to build healthy habits in people's lives, the two joined forces and moved forward with the project.

Together, Chen and Venticinque began refining their app to help users build a habit of using Fitbod in the gym.

Here's their Hooked Model: After identifying the first

step of their Hook, the internal trigger of uncertainty, Chen and Venticinque needed to ensure Fitbod's action phase would quickly solve the user's psychological need by providing certainty about what they should do in the gym.

I acutely remember the embarrassing feeling of standing around in the gym not knowing what to do, and feeling I was probably in someone's way. With Fitbod, simply opening the app provides quick relief.

With one tap on the app, Fitbod creates my next workout, removing the discomfort of uncertainty by quickly telling me which exercises to do, in what order, how much weight to lift, how many repetitions to do, and even how long to rest between sets. I don't have to think about anything. I just have to do what Fitbod tells me to do. "The simplicity of a single 'next workout to do' really helps the gym-goer quickly solve their psychological uncertainty," Venticinque told me (figure 34).[9]

By generating the workout program on the fly, Fitbod overcomes some of the stumbling blocks associated with other fitness programs. For instance, whereas most of Fitbod's competitors ask users to embark on a lengthy multiweek program, Fitbod requires no long-term commitments. Similarly, if users fall off track, they can easily get back on track because the app is always ready with their next best workout.

Next comes the variable reward phase of Fitbod's Hooked Model. Not only is there an element of surprise in discovering which exercises the app chooses for me (rewards of the

hunt), but the app also brings out the intrinsically rewarding elements of exercise as well. Unlike other fitness apps that give users corny badges or points, which can become less motivating over time, the main reward when using Fitbod is the satisfaction of conquering the exercise itself. By giving users clear weight and repetition goals for each activity, Fitbod harnesses the search for mastery and competence endemic to "rewards of the self." There's variability in seeing if you can smash your personal best. And Fitbod helps by setting achievable, incremental goals with each exercise.

Finally, Fitbod gets smarter with use, a characteristic of well-designed, habit-forming products. The investment phase of Fitbod's Hooked Model occurs every time I log an exercise. By entering data, I'm storing value in the service and ensuring it improves the more I use it. With my previous exercise information, the app tailors future sessions and recommendations. I can also invest more value in the app by tailoring my fitness goals, available equipment, and even how much time I have to work out—all factors the app uses to compute my next tailored workout.

Fitbod isn't free. Users pay a monthly or annual subscription. But unlike gym memberships, which most people abandon despite continuing to pay dues, the Fitbod founders tell me their app loses very few customers and is used on average nine times per month per user. Fitbod's application of the Hooked Model is clearly working. The founders tell me its user base and profits continue to grow.

As someone who has always struggled with inconsistent exercising habits, I'm proud to say that I've formed an indispensable habit with Fitbod. I'm happy to let the app do the thinking for me so I can focus on my workout. Instead of relying on an expensive personal trainer or spending countless hours reading fitness books and logging exercises with clunky pen and paper, I've finally built a helpful and healthy habit.

REMEMBER & SHARE

- After reading *Hooked*, the founders of the Fitbod App targeted a very specific user habit.

- Unlike competitors who went after vague behaviors like "build a healthy lifestyle," Fitbod sought to own the internal trigger related to the uncomfortable feeling of uncertainty of not knowing what to do in the gym.

- Fitbod's action phase quickly solves the user's psychological discomfort by providing very specific instructions with a single tap of the app.

- In Fitbod's variable rewards phase, discover which exercise to do, how much weight to lift, and how many repetitions to complete to beat their personal best.

- Finally, the data users enter when they complete an exercise improves the service and loads the next external trigger, thus perpetuating the habit of using the app.

| 8 |

Habit Testing and Where to Look for Habit-Forming Opportunities

Now that you have an understanding of the Hooked Model and have reflected on the morality of influencing user behavior, it is time to get to work. Running your idea through the four phases of the model will help you discover potential weaknesses in your product's habit-forming potential.

Does your users' internal trigger frequently prompt them to action? Is your external trigger cueing them when they are most likely to act? Is your design simple enough to make taking the action easy? Does the reward satisfy your users' need while leaving them wanting more? Do your users invest a bit of work in the product, storing value to improve the experience with use and loading the next trigger?

By identifying where your product or service is lacking, you can focus on developing improvements to your product where it matters most.

Habit Testing

By following the "Do This Now" sections in previous chapters, you should have enough knowledge to prototype your product. But simply coming up with ideas is not enough, and creating user habits is often easier said than done. The process of developing successful habit-forming technologies requires patience and persistence.

The Hooked Model can be a helpful tool for filtering out bad ideas with low habit potential as well as a framework for identifying room for improvement in existing products.

However, after the designer has formulated new hypotheses, there is no way to know which ideas will work without testing them with actual users.

Building a habit-forming product is an iterative process and requires user-behavior analysis and continuous experimentation.

How can you implement the concepts in this book to measure your product's effectiveness in building user habits?

Through my studies and discussions with entrepreneurs at today's most successful habit-forming companies, I've distilled this process into what I term *Habit Testing*. It is a process inspired by the "build, measure, learn" methodology championed by the lean start-up movement. Habit Testing offers insights and actionable data to inform the design of habit-forming products. It helps clarify who your devotees are, what parts (if any) of your product are habit forming, and why those aspects of your product are changing user behavior.

Habit Testing does not always require a live product; however, it can be difficult to draw clear conclusions without a comprehensive view of how people are using your system. The following steps assume you have a product, users, and meaningful data to explore.

Step 1: Identify

The initial question for Habit Testing is "Who are the product's habitual users?" Remember, the more frequently your product is used, the more likely it is to form a user habit.

> *First, define what it means to be a* devoted user. *How often "should" one use your product?*

The answer to this question is very important and can widely change your perspective. Publicly available data from similar products or solutions can help define your users and engagement targets. If data are not available, educated assumptions must be made—but be realistic and honest.

If you are building a social networking app like Slack or Instagram, you should expect habitual users to visit the service multiple times per day. On the other hand, you should not expect users of a movie recommendation site like

Rotten Tomatoes to visit more than once or twice a week (because their visits will come on the heels of seeing a movie or researching one to watch). Don't come up with an overly aggressive prediction that only accounts for überusers; you are looking for a realistic guess to calibrate how often typical users will interact with your product.

Once you know how often users *should* use your product, dig into the numbers to identify how many and which type of users meet this threshold. As a best practice, use cohort analysis to measure changes in user behavior through future product iterations.

Step 2: Codify

Let's say that you've identified a few users who meet the criteria of habitual users. Yet how many such users are enough? My rule of thumb is 5 percent. Though your rate of active users will need to be much higher to sustain your business, this is a good initial benchmark.

However, if at least 5 percent of your users don't find your product valuable enough to use as much as you predicted they would, you may have a problem. Either you identified the wrong users or your product needs to go back to the drawing board. If you have exceeded that bar, though, and identified your habitual users, the next step is to codify the steps they took using your product to understand what hooked them.

Users will interact with your product in slightly different ways. Even if you have a standard user flow, the way users engage with your product creates a unique fingerprint. Where users are coming from, decisions made when registering, and the number of friends using the service are just a few of the behaviors that help create a recognizable pattern. Sift through the data to determine if similarities emerge.

> *You are looking for a* Habit Path—*a series of similar actions shared by your most loyal users.*

For example, in its early days, Twitter discovered that once new users followed thirty other members, they hit a tipping point that dramatically increased the odds they would keep using the site.[1]

Every product has a different set of actions that devoted users take; the goal of finding the Habit Path is to determine which of these steps is critical for creating devoted users so that you can modify the experience to encourage this behavior.

Step 3: Modify

Armed with new insights, it is time to revisit your product and identify ways to nudge new users down the same Habit Path taken by devotees. This may include an update to the registration funnel, content changes, feature removal, or increased emphasis on an existing feature. Twitter used the insights gained from the previous step to modify its on-boarding process, encouraging new users to immediately begin following others.

Habit Testing is a continual process you can implement with every new feature and product iteration.

Tracking users by cohort and comparing their activity with that of habitual users should guide how products evolve and improve.

Discovering Habit-forming Opportunities

The Habit Testing process requires the product designer to have an existing product to test. Where, though, might you look to find potentially habit-forming experiences ripe for new technological solutions?

When it comes to developing new products, there are no guarantees. Along with creating an engaging product as described in this book, start-ups must also find a way to monetize and grow. Although this book does not cover business models for delivering customer value or methods for profitable customer acquisition, both are necessary components of any successful business. Several things must go right for a new company to succeed, and forming user habits is just one of them.

As we saw in chapter 6, being a facilitator is not only a moral imperative, it also makes for better businesses practices. Creating a product the designer uses and believes materially improves people's lives increases the odds of delivering something people want. Therefore, the first place for the entrepreneur or designer to look for new opportunities is in the mirror.

Paul Graham advises entrepreneurs to leave the sexy-sounding business ideas behind and instead build for their own needs: "Instead of asking 'what problem should I solve?' ask 'what problem do I wish someone else would solve for me?'"[2]

Studying your own needs can lead to remarkable discoveries and new ideas because the designer always has a direct line to at least one user: him- or herself.

For example, Buffer, a service for posting updates to social networks, was inspired by its founder's insightful observations of his own behavior.

Buffer was founded in 2010 and is now used by over 1.1 million people.[3] Its founder, Joel Gascoigne, described the company's inception in an interview.[4] "The idea for Buffer came to me after I had been using Twitter for about 1.5 years. I had started to share links to blog posts and quotes I found inspiring, and I found that my followers seemed to really like these types of tweets. I would often get retweets or end up having a great conversation around the blog post or quote. That's when I decided I wanted to share this kind of content more frequently, because the conversations being triggered were allowing me to be in touch with some super smart and interesting people."

Gascoigne continues, "So, with my goal of sharing more blog posts and quotes, I started to do it manually. I quickly realized that it would be far more efficient to schedule these tweets for the future, so I started to use a few available

Twitter clients to do this. The key pain I ran into here was that I would have to choose the exact date and time for the tweet, and in reality all I wanted to do was to tweet 'five times per day.' I just wanted the tweets to be spread out so I didn't share them all at the same time when I did my daily reading. For a while, I used a notepad and kept track of when I had scheduled tweets, so that I could try and tweet five times per day. This became quite cumbersome, and so my idea was born: I wanted to make scheduling tweets 'x times a day' as easy as tweeting regularly."

Gascoigne's story is a classic example of a founder scratching his own itch. As he used existing solutions, he recognized a discrepancy in what they offered and the solution he needed. He identified where steps could be removed from other products he used and built a simpler way to get his job done.

Careful introspection can uncover opportunities for building habit-forming products.

> *As you go about your day, ask yourself why you do or do not do certain things and how those tasks could be made easier or more rewarding.*

Observing your own behavior can inspire the next habit-forming product or inform a breakthrough improvement to an existing solution. Read on to find other hotbeds for innovation opportunities—think of them as shortcuts for uncovering existing behaviors that are ripe for successful business development based on forming new user habits.

Nascent Behaviors

Sometimes technologies that appear to cater to a niche will cross into the mainstream. Behaviors that start with a small group of users can expand to a wider population, but only if they cater to a broad need. However, the fact that the technology is at first used only by a small population often deceives observers into dismissing the product's true potential.

A striking number of world-changing innovations were written off as mere novelties with limited commercial appeal. George Eastman's Brownie camera, preloaded with a film roll and selling for just $1, was originally marketed as a child's toy.[5] Established studio photographers saw the device as little more than a cheap plaything.

The invention of the telephone was also dismissed at first. Sir William Henry Preece, the chief engineer of the British post office, famously declared, "The Americans have need of the telephone, but we do not. We have plenty of messenger boys."[6]

In 1911 Ferdinand Foch, the future commander in chief of the Allied forces in World War I, said, "Airplanes are interesting toys but of no military value."[7]

In 1957 the editor of business books for Prentice Hall told his publisher, "I have traveled the length and breadth of this country and talked with the best people, and I can assure you that data processing is a fad that won't last out the year."

The Internet itself, and each successive wave of innovation, has continually received criticism for its inability to gain mass appeal. In 1995 Clifford Stoll wrote a *Newsweek* article, "The Internet? Bah!" in which he declared, "The truth is no online database will replace your daily newspaper." Stoll continued, "We'll soon buy books and newspapers straight over the Internet. Uh, sure."[8]

Naturally, now we do read books and newspapers over the Internet. When technologies are new, people are often skeptical. Old habits die hard and few people have the foresight to see how new innovations will eventually change their routines. However, by looking to early adopters who have already developed nascent behaviors, entrepreneurs and designers can identify niche use cases, which can be taken mainstream.

For example, in its early days, Facebook was only used by Harvard students. The service mimicked an off-line behavior familiar to all college students at the time: perusing a printed book of student faces and profiles. After finding popularity at Harvard, Facebook rolled out to other Ivy League schools, then to college students nationwide. Next came high school kids and later, employees at select companies. Finally, in September 2006, Facebook was opened to the world. Currently, over two billion people use Facebook. What first began as a nascent behavior at one campus became a global phenomenon catering to the fundamental human need for connection to others.

As discussed in the first chapter, many habit-forming technologies begin as vitamins—nice-to-have products that, over time, become must-have painkillers by relieving an itch or pain. It is revealing that so many breakthrough technologies and companies, from airplanes to Airbnb, were at first dismissed by critics as toys or niche markets. Looking for nascent behaviors among early adopters can often uncover valuable new business opportunities.

Enabling Technologies

Mike Maples Jr., a Silicon Valley "super angel" investor, likens technology to big-wave surfing. In 2012 Maples blogged, "In my experience, every decade or so, we see a major new tech wave. When I was in high school, it was the PC revolution. I made my career as an entrepreneur at the end of the client/server wave and in the early phases of the Internet wave. Today, we are at the mass adoption phase of the social networking wave. I am obsessed with these technology waves and have spent a lot of time studying how they develop and what patterns can be observed."

Maples believes technology waves follow a three-phase pattern: "They start with infrastructure. Advances in infrastructure are the preliminary forces that enable a large wave to gather. As the wave begins to gather, enabling technologies and platforms create the basis for new types of applications that cause a gathering wave to achieve massive penetration and customer adoption. Eventually, these waves crest and subside, making way for the next gathering wave to take shape."[9]

Entrepreneurs looking for windows of opportunity would be wise to consider Maples's metaphor.

Wherever new technologies suddenly make a behavior easier, new possibilities are born.

The creation of a new infrastructure often opens up unforeseen ways to make other actions simpler or more rewarding. For example, the Internet was first made possible because of the infrastructure commissioned by the U.S. government during the cold war. Next, enabling technologies such as dial-up modems, followed by high-speed Internet connections, provided access to the web. Finally, HTML, web browsers, and search engines—the application layer—made browsing possible on the World Wide Web. At each successive stage, previous enabling technologies allowed new behaviors and businesses to flourish.

Identifying areas where a new technology makes cycling through the Hooked Model faster, more frequent, or more rewarding provides fertile ground for developing new habit-forming products.

Interface Change

Technological changes often create opportunities to build new hooks. However, sometimes no technology change is required.

Many companies have found success in driving new habit formation by identifying how changing user interactions can create new routines.

Whenever a massive change occurs in the way people interact with technology, expect to find plenty of opportunities ripe for harvesting. Changes in interface suddenly make all sorts of behaviors easier. Subsequently, when the effort required to accomplish an action decreases, usage tends to explode.

A long history of technology businesses earned their fortunes discovering behavioral secrets made visible because of a change in the interface. Apple and Microsoft succeeded by turning clunky terminals into graphical user interfaces (GUI) accessible by mainstream consumers. Google simplified the search interface as compared with those of ad-heavy, difficult-to-use competitors such as Yahoo! and Lycos. Facebook and Twitter turned new behavioral insights into interfaces that simplified social interactions online. In each case, a new interface made an action easier and uncovered surprising truths about user behaviors.

More recently, Instagram and Pinterest have capitalized on behavioral insights brought about by interface changes. Pinterest's ability to create a rich canvas of images—utilizing what were then cutting-edge interface changes—revealed new insights about the addictive nature of an online catalog. For Instagram, the interface change was cameras integrated into smartphones. Instagram discovered that its low-tech filters made relatively poor-quality smartphone photos look great. Suddenly taking good pictures with your phone was easier; Instagram used its newly discovered insights to recruit an army of rabidly snapping users. With both Pinterest and

Instagram, tiny teams generated huge value—not by cracking hard technical challenges, but by solving common interaction problems. Likewise, the fast ascent of mobile devices, including tablets, has spawned a new revolution in interface changes—and a new generation of start-up products and services designed around mobile user needs and behaviors.

To uncover where interfaces are changing, Paul Buchheit, a partner at Y Combinator, encourages entrepreneurs to "live in the future."[10] A profusion of interface changes are just a few years away. Wearable technologies like the Apple Watch, the Oculus Rift virtual reality goggles, and Amazon's Echo promise to change how users interact with the real and digital worlds. By looking forward to anticipate where interfaces will change, the enterprising designer can uncover new ways to form user habits.

REMEMBER & SHARE

- The Hooked Model helps the product designer generate an initial prototype for a habit-forming technology. It also helps uncover potential weaknesses in an existing product's habit-forming potential.

- Once a product is built, *Habit Testing* helps uncover product devotees, discover which product elements (if any) are habit forming, and why those aspects of your product change user behavior. Habit Testing includes three steps: *identify*, *codify*, and *modify*.

- First, dig into the data to *identify* how people are using the product.

- Next, *codify* these findings in search of habitual users. To generate new hypotheses, study the actions and paths taken by devoted users.

- Finally, *modify* the product to influence more users to follow the same path as your habitual users, and then evaluate results and continue to modify as needed.

- Keen observation of one's own behavior can lead to new insights and habit-forming product opportunities.

- Identifying areas where a new technology makes cycling through the Hooked Model faster, more frequent, or more rewarding provides fertile ground for developing new habit-forming products.

- *Nascent behaviors*—new behaviors that few people see or do, yet ultimately fulfill a mass-market need—can inform future breakthrough habit-forming opportunities.

- New interfaces lead to transformative behavior change and business opportunities.

DO THIS NOW

Refer to the answers you came up with in the "Do This Now" section in chapter 5 to complete the following exercises:

- Perform Habit Testing, as described in this chapter, to identify the steps users take toward long-term engagement.

- Be aware of your behaviors and emotions for the next week as you use everyday products. Ask yourself:

  - What triggered me to use these products? Was I prompted externally or through internal means?

  - Am I using these products as intended?

  - How might these products improve their onboarding funnels, reengage users through additional external triggers, or encourage users to invest in their services?

- Speak with three people outside your social circle to discover which apps occupy the first screen on their mobile devices. Ask them to use these apps as they normally would and see if you uncover any unnecessary or nascent behaviors.

- Brainstorm five new interfaces that could introduce opportunities or threats to your business.

|bonus content|

Thank you for investing in this book. Now that you have read it, I hope you'll put these practices to good use.

I have free bonus content waiting for you, including a supplementary workbook, product psychology e-mail course, and videos about building habit-forming products.

Visit NirAndFar.com/Hooked for this content.

Also, it would mean so much to me if you could take a moment to review the book online, "but you are free to accept or refuse." ☺

Amazon—NirAndFar.com/GetHooked

Goodreads—goo.gl/UBHeLY

Be sure to visit my blog, NirAndFar.com, to learn more about habit-forming products and receive my latest essays.

Finally, please send questions, comments, edits, or feedback to NirAndFar.com/Contact.

Thank you and please let me know how you use habits for good!

acknowledgments

If I am ever asked, "What was the most surprising thing you learned while writing this book?" I won't respond with any of the research studies or company examples you've read. Although the topic has captivated me for over two and a half years, there can be only one answer to this question: I never knew how generous people could be.

I owe a particular debt of gratitude to the following people. This book truly would not have been possible without them.

Michelle Ahronovitz, Stephen Anderson, Dan Ariely, Jess Bachman, Gil Ben-Artzy, Laura Bergheim, Jonathan Bolden, Michal Bortnik, Vlada Bortnik, Ramsay Brown, James Cham, Tim Chang, Andrew Chen, Sangeet Paul Choudary, Steve Corcoran, Alex Cowan, John Dailey, Tanna Drapkin, Karen Dulski, Scott Dunlap, Eric Eldon, Josh Elman, Jasmine Eyal, Monique Eyal, Ofir Eyal, Omer Eyal, Ronit Eyal, Victor Eyal, Andrew Feiler, Christy Fletcher, B. J. Fogg, Janice Fraser, Jason Fraser, Shuly Galili, Ben Gardner, Kelly Greenwood, Bobby Gruenewald, Jonathan Guerrera, Austin Gunter, Steph Habif, Leslie Harlson, Stephen Houghton, Jason Hreha, Gabriela

Hromis, Peter Jackson, Noah Kagan, Dave Kashen, Amy Jo Kim, John Kim, Michael Kim, David King, Thomas Kjemperud, Tristan Kromer, Rok Krulec, Michal Levin, Jonathan Libov, Chuck Longanecker and the team at Digital Telepathy, Jennifer Lu, Wayne Lue, Jules Maltz, Zack Marom, Dave McClure, Kelly McGonigal, Sarah Melnyk, Oreon Mounter and the team at Moment Communications Inc., Matt Mullenweg, Yash Nelapati, David Ngo, Thomas O'Duffy, Max Ogles, Amy O'Leary, Line Oma, Alex Osterwalder, Trevor Owens, Niki Papadopoulos, Brett Redinger, Sharbani Roy, Gretchen Rubin, Lisa Rutherford, Kate Rutter, Paul Sas, Todd Sattersten, Travis Sentell, Bhavin Shah, Hiten Shah, Jason Shen, Baba Shiv, Rebecca Shoenthal, Paul Singh, Katja Spreckelmeyer, Jon Stone, Nisha Sudarsanam, Lydia Sugarman, Tim Sullivan, Tracey Sullivan, Guy Vincent, Jeff Waldstreicher, Charles Wang, AnneMarie Ward, Stephen Wendell, Mark Williamson, David Wolfe, Colin Zhu, Gabe Zichermann.

There are two more people who deserve extra recognition: First, Ryan Hoover, the contributing author, was instrumental in helping me turn a jumble of blog posts and writing scraps into a cohesive book. His dedication to this project, writing talent, and dogged persistence made the idea of this book a reality. I am sure the world will be hearing much more from Ryan in the years to come and I feel fortunate to have worked with him early in his career.

Next, this book is dedicated to my wife, Julie Li-Eyal. Julie assisted with everything, from practical tasks (such as designing the book cover and presentation slides) to serving as a sounding board during the ups and downs of the writing process. However, of all her contributions, the greatest is her unwavering support. Her endless affection leaves me forever in her debt and always wondering how I got so lucky.

Contributors

Thank you to the loyal blog subscribers who provided insightful feedback, careful edits, moral support, and gentle prodding.

The people listed on the following pages donated their time and insights to improving this book. I am in awe of their willingness to contribute to making this book what it is.

Shira Abel

Ashita Achuthan

Géraldine Adams

Buki Adeniji

Anuj Adhiya

Akash Agarwal

Michael Agnich

Payam Ahangar

Charles Ajidahun

Adi Alhadeff

Bashar Al-Nakhala

Colt Alton

Dina Amin

Preet Anand

Margaret Ancobiah

Ravikiran Annaswamy

Lauri Antalainen

Nikola Arabadjiev

Steve Arnold

Conall Arora

George Arutyunyan

Sunil Arvindam

Eldad Askof

Taimur Aslam

Nadya Averkieva

Mark Avnet

Hazem Awad

Paul Baccaro

Deepak Baid

Courtney Baker

Gary Baker

Paul Ballas

Jennifer Baloian

Naren Bansal

Jenny Barnes

Anat Baron

Matthew Barry

Neal Battaglia

Brian Bell

Simon Bentholm

Tim Benwell

Hampus Bergqvist

Brian Bettendorf

Ajay Bharadwaj

Maggie Biggs

Brad Birt

Justin Blanchard

Jim Bloedau

Sean Boisen

Jason Brady

Johan Brand

Jamie Bresner

Brendan Brown

Ramsay Brown

Robert Brown

Sarah E. Brown

Piotr Bucki

Ella Buitenman

Josip Bujas

Gabriela Cándano Herbas

Marica Caposaldo

Christopher Carfi

Jon Carr-Harris

Kevin Carroll

Giuseppe Catalfamo

Yoonji Chae

Ora Chaiken

Jacky Chan

Dennis Chandler

Kathy Chang

Stephen Chang

Geeta Chauhan

Sylvia Chebi

Frank Chen

Lucy Chen

Zhongning Chen

Chikodi Chima

Vivek Chopra

Sangeet Paul Choudary

Scott Christ

Yannis Christopoulos

Eugene Chuvyrov

Fran Civile

Gillian Clowes

Armin Čobo

Victor Colombo

Jim Conaghan

Esteban Contreras

Jacob Cook

Justin Copeland

Maxime Cormier

Ben Cote

Sylvia Creswell

Hana Crume

Andrian Cucu

Steve Cunningham

Antonio D'souza

Diogo da Silva

Steven Daar

Hadiyah Daché

Chad Dahlstrom

David Datny

Deeti Dave

David Davenport-Firth

Detrick DeBurr

Bart Denny

Shai Desai

Simren S. Dhaliwal

Cassius Dhelon

CASUDI aka Caroline Di Diego

António Dias

Andre Dickson

Andrew Didenko

Shawn Dimantha

Peter Dimitrov

Richard Dinerman

Florian Disson

Nolan Dubeau

Denise Duffy

Scott Dunlap

Arkadiusz Dymalski

Lars Eickmeier

André Eilertsen

Eyal Eldar

Dagur Eyjolfsson

Kingsley Ezejiaku

Fred Farnam

Pierre-Emile Faroult

Jack Farrell

Lloyd Fassett

Mijael Feldman

Yoel Feldman

Francesco Ferrazzino

Tony Fish

David Flemate

Keith Fleming

Joel Frisch

Timo Fritsche

Kaoru Fujita

Benjamin Gadbaw

Uli Gal-Oz

Hari Ganapathy

Amir Ganjeii

Magne Matre Gåsland

Meghbartma Gautam

Melissa Gena

Sigal Geshury

Sajad Ghanizada

Drew Gierach

Endri Gjinushi

Anshu Goel

Ming Gong

Pedro L. González

Jason Grace

Charlie Gragam

David Gratton

Ravishankar Gundlapalli

Abhishek Gupta

Michael Haberman

Steph Habif

Rob Hall

Hadas Hamerovv

Albert Hartman

Ebrahim-Khalil Hassen

Eva Hasson

Chris Hawley

Mark Hayes

Elisa Heiken

Alfan Hendro

Benjamin Hoffman

Ryan Holdeman

Jason Holderness

Bob Holling

Joakim Holmquist

Kyle Homstead

Rahul Horé

Jonathan Hoss

Patrick Huitema

Matt Hurley

Nigel Ingham

Christos Iosifidis

Jan Isakovic

Yair Itzhaik

Ranjan Jagannathan

Javid Jamae

Kyle Jaster

Anandan Jayaraman

Eoghan Jennings

Amit Joshipura

Jonathan Kalinowski

Michael Kampff

Dave Kashen

Joshua Keay

Chandra Keith

Jason Kende

Gary Kind

Ed King

Jason King

Marcia Kinstler

Thomas Kjemperud

Michael Klazema

Tobias Kluge

Russ Klusas

Kathleen Knopoff

Felix Köbler

Vadim Komisarchik

R George Komoto

Jonathan Korn

Ravi Kotichintala

Mohammed Kromah

Charlie Kubal

Vineesh Kumar

Chris Kurdziel

Tim Kutnick

Brooks Lambert

Brian Lance

Betsy Lane

Norman Law

Vinney Le

Sebastien Le Tuan

Cody Lee

Rudi Leismann

Stephanie Lenorovitz

Andrew Levy

Anson Liang

Marvin Liao

Roland Ligtenberg

Eyal Livne

Tobias Loerracher

Jenn Lonzer

Jeff Lougheed

Jennifer Lu

Paul Lucas

Waynn Lue

Ricardo Luevanos Jr.

Ivan Lukianchuk

Pavan Lulla

Morten Lundsby

Darren Luvaas

Amanda MacArthur

Murray Macdonald

Churchill Madyavanhu

Jay Chuck Mailen

Solene Maitre

Wes Maldonado

Stanislav Maleshkov

Craig Mankelow

Armando Mann

Alexander Manolov

Jerad Maplethorpe

Angelos Marantos

Ivan Markovic

Leon Markovitz

Alon Matas

Chris Mathew

Jonathan Matus

Sunil Maulik

Gavin McDermott

Jon McGee

Michael McGee

Gilberto Medrano

Alfons Mencke

Aadesh Midtry

Christopher Miles

Greg Miliatis

Sophie-Charlotte Moatti

Lindsey Moav

Joe Mocquant

Pranoy Modi

Peter Monien

Aaron Moore

Thomas Morselt

Kareem Mostafa

Jodie Moule

Olivia Muesse

Tim Mukata

Noel Mulkeen

Lee Munroe

Neil Murray

Nikhil Nadkarni

Szabolcs Nagy

Nitya Narasimhan

Amaan Nathoo

Basanth Kumar Neeli

Errol Nezar

Vas Nikolaev

Dawn Novarina

Thomas O'Duffy

Neal O'Gorman

Sean O'Leary

Seyi Ogunyemi

Oli Olsen

Steve Omohundro

Kevin Ondyak

Alfredo Osorio

Ambika Pajjuri

Peter Pallotta

Hesam Panahi

Felipe Escanilla Panza

Petar Papikj

Juan Paredes

Lance Parker

Devang Patel

Nipul Patel

Randy Paynter

Allan Pedersen

Paolo Perazzo

Gary Percy

Igal Perelman

Daniele Peron

Nicholas Peterson

Jean-Baptiste Pin

Stephan Plesnik

Justin Pollard

Vera Polyakova

Eike Post

Dr. Eike Berend Post

Gilles Poupardin

Chris Pousset

Gee Powell

Mikhail Pozin

Julie Price

Amala Putrevu

Maniappan R.

Christian Raaby

Moshik Raccah

Cyrus Radfar

Sanjay Radhakrishnan

Brett Radlicki

Claudine Felice Ramirez

Umesh Rangappa

Ritesh Ranjan

Tore Rasmussen

Zoheb Raza

Christi Reid

Ophir Reshef

Kamil Rextin

Justin Reyes

Steve Rigell

Edson Rigonatti

Billy Robins

Lior Romano

Johann Romefort

Shai Rosen

Megan Rounds

Mark Rowland

Steve Rowling

Leon Rubinstein

Emily Ryan

Ari Salomon

Oren Samari

Julius Sapoka

Steven Saunders

Sid Savara

Adele Savarese

Amol Saxena

Matt Schaar

Charles Schaefer

Rick Schaefer

Miranda Schenkel

Nati Mark Schlesinger

Willemijn Schmitz

Johannes Schneider

Jason Schwartz

Adrian Scott

Joel Scott

Mark Sefaradi

Cameron Sepah

Sharad Seth

Rajesh Setty

Francisco Sevillano

Bhavin Shah

Sarah Shaiq

Aviv Shalgi

Yaron Shapira

Neeraj Sharma

Priya Sheth

Kevin Shin

Timothy Shipman

John Shoffner

Barak Shragai

Michael Siepmann

Diogo Silva

Michael Simpson

Navarjun Singh

Rachna Singh

Raj Singh

Indra Singhal

Chris Sluz

Dana Smith

Nick Soman

Matthew Sonier

Adam Sowers

Jonathan Squires

Karthik Srinivasan

John Starmer

Slobodan Stipic

Aleksandar Stojanovic

Dave Stone

Nisha Sudarsanam

Lydia Sugarman

Mike Summerfield

Andreas Sutharia

Brent Taggart

Itai Talmi

Dixit Talwar

Michael Tame

Norman Tan

Eva Tang

Ali Rushdan Tariq

John Thompson

Bob Thordarson

Brenton Thornicroft

Barbara Tien

Amir Toister

Jacqueline Tomko

Andrea Torino-Rodriguez

Raul Troyo

Steph Tryphonas

Rattapoom Tuchinda

Oji Udezue

Cristobal Undurraga

Adriana Ursache

Haruna Usman

Branislav Vajagić

Paul Valcheff

Joeri Vankeirsbilck

Tim Varner

Ashwanth Vemulapalli

René Vendrig

Francisco Vieyra

Alberto Villa

Guy Vincent

Khuong Vo Thanh

Marcus Vorwaller

Todd Wahnish

Akane Wakasugi

Karl Waldman

AnneMarie Ward

Mark Warren

Alan Weinkrant

Jay Weintraub

Stephen Wendel

Erik Wesslen

Albert Wieringa

Denis Wilson
Rick Winfield
Melinda Wiria
Reggie Wirjadi
Vanita Wolf
Nathanael Wolfe
Lyon Wong
Margo Wright
Renee Yarbrough
Dean Young

Beverley Zabow
Danny Zagorski
Hasnain Zaheer
Cindy Ris Zanca
Xin Zhou
Julie Zilber
Tal Zilberman
Keivan Zolfaghari
Zoran Zuber

|notes|

Introduction

1. "Always Connected: How Smartphones and Social Keep Us Engaged," IDC-Facebook (accessed Dec. 19, 2013), https://www.nu.nl/files/IDC-Facebook%20Always%20Connected%20(1).pdf.

2. "Survey Finds One-Third of Americans More Willing to Give Up Sex Than Their Mobile Phones," TeleNav (accessed Dec. 19, 2013), http://www.telenav.com/about/pr-summer-travel/report-20110803.html.

3. Antti Oulasvirta, Tye Rattenbury, Lingyi Ma, and Eeva Raita, "Habits Make Smartphone Use More Pervasive," *Personal and Ubiquitous Computing* 16, no. 1 (Jan. 2012): 105–14, doi:10.1007/s00779-011-0412-2.

4. Dusan Belic, "Tomi Ahonen: Average Users Looks at Their Phone 150 Times a Day!" *IntoMobile* (accessed Dec. 19, 2013), http://www.intomobile.com/2012/02/09/tomi-ahonen-average-users-looks-their-phone-150-times-day.

5. E. Morsella, J. A. Bargh, P. M. Gollwitzer, eds., *Oxford Handbook of Human Action* (New York: Oxford University Press, 2008).

6. For purposes of this book, I use the definition of *habit formation* as the process of learning new behaviors through repetition until they become automatic. I am grateful to Dr. Stephen

Wendel for pointing out the spectrum of habits. For a framework describing other automatic behaviors, see: John A. Bargh, "The Four Horsemen of Automaticity: Awareness, Intention, Efficiency, and Control in Social Cognition." *Handbook of Social Cognition*, vol. 1: *Basic Processes*; vol. 2: *Applications* (2nd ed.), eds. R. S. Wyer and T. K. Srull (Hillsdale, NJ: Lawrence Erlbaum Associates, Inc., 1994), 1–40.

7. Bas Verplanken and Wendy Wood, "Interventions to Break and Create Consumer Habits," *Journal of Public Policy & Marketing* 25, no. 1 (March 2006): 90–103, doi:10.1509/jppm .25.1.90.

8. W. Wood and D. T. Neal, "A New Look at Habits and the Habit-Goal Interface," *Psychological Review* 114, no. 4 (2007): 843–63.

9. "Pinterest," Crunchbase, June 25, 2014. http://www.crunch base.com/organization/pinterest.

10. "What Causes Behavior Change?" B. J. Fogg's Behavior Model (accessed Nov. 12, 2013), http://www.behaviormodel.org.

11. "Robert Sapolsky: Are Humans Just Another Primate?" FORA .tv (accessed Dec. 19, 2013), http://fora.tv/2011/02/15/Robert _Sapolsky_Are_Humans_Just_Another_Primate.

12. Damien Brevers and Xavier Noël, "Pathological Gambling and the Loss of Willpower: A Neurocognitive Perspective," *Socioaffective Neuroscience & Psychology* 3, no. 2 (Sept. 2013), doi:10.3402 /snp.v3i0.21592.

13. Paul Graham, "The Acceleration of Addictiveness," (accessed Nov. 12, 2013), http://www.paulgraham.com/addiction.html.

14. *Night of the Living Dead*, IMDb (accessed June 25, 2014), http:// www.imdb.com/title/tt0063350.

15. Richard H. Thaler, Cass R. Sunstein, and John P. Balz, "Choice Architecture" (SSRN Scholarly Paper, Rochester, NY), *Social Science Research Network* (April 2, 2010), http://papers.ssrn .com/abstract=1583509.

Chapter 1: The Habit Zone

1. Wendy Wood, Jeffrey M. Quinn, and Deborah A. Kashy, "Habits in Everyday Life: Thought, Emotion, and Action," *Journal of Personality and Social Psychology* 83, no. 6 (Dec. 2002): 1281–97.

2. Henry H. and Barbara J. Knowlton, "The Role of the Basal Ganglia in Habit Formation," *Nature Reviews Neuroscience* 7, no. 6 (June 2006): 464–76, doi:10.1038/nrn1919.

3. A. Dickinson and B. Balleine, "The Role of Learning in the Operation of Motivational Systems," in C. R. Gallistel (ed.), *Stevens' Handbook of Experimental Psychology: Learning, Motivation, and Emotion* (New York: Wiley and Sons, 2002), 497–534.

4. "Notes from 2005 Berkshire Hathaway Annual Meeting," Tilson Funds (accessed Nov. 12, 2013), http://www.tilsonfunds .com/brkmtg05notes.pdf.

5. "Charlie Munger: Turning $2 Million Into $2 Trillion," *Mungerisms* (accessed Nov. 12, 2013), http://mungerisms.blogspot.com /2010/04/charlie-munger-turning-2-million-into-2.html.

6. "Candy Crush: So Popular It's Killing King's IPO?" *Yahoo Finance* (accessed Dec. 16, 2013), http://finance.yahoo.com /blogs/the-exchange/candy-crush-so-popular-it-s-smashing -interest-in-an-ipo-160523940.html.

7. David Skok, "Lessons Learned—Viral Marketing," *For Entrepreneurs* (accessed Nov. 12, 2013), http://www.forentrepreneurs .com/lessons-learnt-viral-marketing.

8. John T. Gourville, "Eager Sellers and Stony Buyers: Under-standing the Psychology of New-Product Adoption," *Harvard Business Review* (accessed Nov, 12, 2013), http://hbr.org/product /eager-sellers-and-stony-buyers-understanding-the-p/an /R0606F-PDF-ENG.

9. Cecil Adams, "Was the QWERTY Keyboard Purposely De-signed to Slow Typists?," *Straight Dope* (Oct. 30, 1981), http:// www.straightdope.com/columns/read/221/was-the-qwerty -keyboard-purposely-designed-to-slow-typists.

10. Mark E. Bouton, "Context and Behavioral Processes in Extinction," *Learning & Memory* 11, no. 5 (Sept. 2004): 485–94, doi:10.1101/lm.78804.

11. Ari P. Kirshenbaum, Darlene M. Olsen, and Warren K. Bickel, "A Quantitative Review of the Ubiquitous Relapse Curve," *Journal of Substance Abuse Treatment* 36, no. 1 (Jan. 2009): 8–17, doi:10.1016/j.jsat.2008.04.001.

12. Robert W. Jeffery, Leonard H. Epstein, G. Terrence Wilson, Adam Drewnowski, Albert J. Stunkard, and Rena R. Wing, "Long-term Maintenance of Weight Loss: Current Status," *Health Psychology* 19, no. 1 (2000): 5–16, doi:10.1037/0278-6133.19.Suppl1.5.

13. Charles Duhigg, *The Power of Habit: Why We Do What We Do in Life and Business* (New York: Random House, 2012), 20.

14. G. Judah, B. Gardner, and R. Aunger, "Forming a Flossing Habit: An Exploratory Study of the Psychological Determi-nants of Habit Formation," *British Journal of Health Psychology* 18 (2013): 338–53.

15. Matt Wallaert, "Bing Your Brain: Test, Then Test Again," *Bing Blogs* (accessed Dec. 16, 2013), http://www.bing.com/blogs

/site_blogs/b/search/archive/2013/02/06/bing-your-brain
-test-then-test-again.aspx.

16. "comScore Releases September 2013 U.S. Search Engine Rank-
ings." comScore, Inc. (accessed Nov. 12, 2013), http://www.com
score.com/Insights/Press_Releases/2013/10/comScore
_Releases_September_2013_US_Search_Engine_Rankings.

17. Amazon Product Ads, Amazon.com (accessed Nov. 12, 2013),
http://services.amazon.com/content/product-ads-on-amazon
.htm/ref=as_left_pads_apa1#!how-it-works.

18. Valerie Trifts and Gerald Häubl, "Information Availability
and Consumer Preference: Can Online Retailers Benefit from
Providing Access to Competitor Price Information?," *Journal of
Consumer Psychology* 2003, 149–59.

19. Nick Wingfield, "More Retailers at Risk of Amazon 'Show-
rooming,'" *Bits* blog (accessed Dec. 16, 2013), http://bits.blogs
.nytimes.com/2013/02/27/more-retailers-at-risk-of-amazon
-showrooming.

20. Brad Stone, *The Everything Store: Jeff Bezos and the Age of Amazon*
(Boston: Little, Brown and Company, 2013).

21. Phillipa Lally, Cornelia H. M. van Jaarsveld, Henry W. W.
Potts, and Jane Wardle, "How Are Habits Formed: Model-
ling Habit Formation in the Real World," *European Journal
of Social Psychology* 40, no. 6 (2010): 998–1009, doi:10.1002
/ejsp.674.

22. Paul A. Offit, "Don't Take Your Vitamins," *New York Times* (June
8, 2013), http://www.nytimes.com/2013/06/09/opinion/sunday
/dont-take-your-vitamins.html.

Chapter 2: Trigger

1. Accessed Nov. 12, 2013, http://instagram.com/press.

2. Emily McCormick, "Instagram Is Estimated to Be Worth More than $100 Billion," *Bloomberg* (June 25, 2018), https://www.bloomberg.com/news/articles/2018-06-25/value-of-facebook-s-instagram-estimated-to-top-100-billion.

3. "Twitter 'Tried to Buy Instagram before Facebook.'" *Telegraph* (April 16, 2012), http://www.telegraph.co.uk/technology/twitter/9206312/Twitter-tried-to-buy-Instagram-before-Facebook.html.

4. Barry Schwartz, *The Paradox of Choice* (New York: Ecco, 2004).

5. Blake Masters, "Peter Thiel's CS183: Startup—Class 2 Notes Essay," *Blake Masters* (April 6, 2012), http://blakemasters.com/post/20582845717/peter-thiels-cs183-startup-class-2-notes-essay.

6. R. Kotikalapudi, S. Chellappan, F. Montgomery, D. Wunsch, and K. Lutzen, "Associating Internet Usage with Depressive Behavior Among College Students," *IEEE Technology and Society Magazine* 31, no. 4 (2012): 73–80, doi:10.1109/MTS.2012.2225462.

7. Sriram Chellappan and Raghavendra Kotikalapudi, "How Depressed People Use the Internet," *New York Times* (June 15, 2012), http://www.nytimes.com/2012/06/17/opinion/sunday/how-depressed-people-use-the-internet.html.

8. Ryan Tate, "Twitter Founder Reveals Secret Formula for Getting Rich Online," *Wired* (accessed Nov. 12, 2013), http://www.wired.com/business/2013/09/ev-williams-xoxo.

9. Erika Hall, "How the 'Failure' Culture of Startups Is Killing Innovation," *Wired* (accessed Nov. 12, 2013), http://www.wired

.com/opinion/2013/09/why-do-research-when-you-can-fail-fast-pivot-and-act-out-other-popular-startup-cliches.

10. "The Power of User Narratives: Jack Dorsey (Square)," video, Entrepreneurial Thought Leaders Lecture (Stanford University, 2011), http://ecorner.stanford.edu/authorMaterialInfo.html?mid=2644.

11. Eric Ries, "What Is Customer Development?," *Startup Lessons Learned* (accessed Nov. 12, 2013), http://www.startuplessonslearned.com/2008/11/what-is-customer-development.html.

12. Rich Crandall, "Empathy Map," the K12 Lab Wiki (accessed Nov. 12, 2013), https://dschool.stanford.edu/groups/k12/wiki/3d994/Empathy_Map.html.

13. Taiichi Ohno, *Toyota Production System: Beyond Large-scale Production* (Portland, OR: Productivity Press, 1988).

14. For more on the need for social belonging, see: Susan T. Fiske, *Social Beings: A Core Motives Approach to Social Psychology* (Hoboken: Wiley, 2010).

Chapter 3: Action

1. "What Causes Behavior Change?," B. J. Fogg's Behavior Model (accessed Nov. 12, 2013), http://behaviormodel.org.

2. Edward L. Deci and Richard M. Ryan, "Self-determination Theory: A Macrotheory of Human Motivation, Development, and Health," *Canadian Psychology/Psychologie Canadienne* 49, no. 3 (2008): 182–85, doi:10.1037/a0012801.

3. Barack Obama "Hope" poster, Wikipedia, the Free Encyclopedia, November 5, 2013, http://en.wikipedia.org/w/index.php?title=Barack_Obama_%22Hope%22_poster&oldid=579742540.

4. Denis J. Hauptly, *Something Really New: Three Simple Steps to Creating Truly Innovative Products* (New York: AMACOM, 2007).

5. Ingrid Lunden, "Analyst: Twitter Passed 500M Users in June 2012, 140M of Them in US; Jakarta 'Biggest Tweeting' City," *TechCrunch* (accessed Nov. 12, 2013), http://techcrunch.com /2012/07/30/analyst-twitter-passed-500m-users-in-june-2012 -140m-of-them-in-us-jakarta-biggest-tweeting-city.

6. "What Causes Behavior Change?," B. J. Fogg's Behavior Model (accessed Nov. 12, 2013), http://www.behaviormodel.org.

7. Leena Rao, "Twitter Seeing 90 Million Tweets Per Day, 25 Percent Contain Links," *TechCrunch* (accessed Nov. 12, 2013), http://techcrunch.com/2010/09/14/twitter-seeing-90-million -tweets-per-day.

8. Stephen Worchel, Jerry Lee, and Akanbi Adewole, "Effects of Supply and Demand on Ratings of Object Value," *Journal of Personality and Social Psychology* 32, no. 5 (1975): 906–14, doi:10.1037 /0022-3514.32.5.906.

9. Gene Weingarten, "Pearls Before Breakfast," *Washington Post* (April 8, 2007), http://www.washingtonpost.com/wp-dyn /content/article/2007/04/04/AR2007040401721.html.

10. Hilke Plassmann, John O'Doherty, Baba Shiv, and Antonio Rangel, "Marketing Actions Can Modulate Neural Representations of Experienced Pleasantness," *Proceedings of the National Academy of Sciences* 105, no. 3 (Jan. 2008): 1050–54, doi:10.1073 /pnas.0706929105.

11. Joseph Nunes and Xavier Dreze, "The Endowed Progress Effect: How Artificial Advancement Increases Effort" (SSRN Scholarly Paper, Rochester, New York), *Social Science Research*

Network (accessed Nov. 12, 2013), http://papers.ssrn.com/abstract=991962.

12. "List of Cognitive Biases," Wikipedia, the Free Encyclopedia (accessed November 12, 2013), http://en.wikipedia.org/wiki/List_of_cognitive_biases.

Chapter 4: Variable Reward

1. J. Olds and P. Milner, "Positive reinforcement produced by electrical stimulation of the septal area and other regions of rat brain," *Journal of Comparative and Physiological Psychology* 47 (1954), 419–27.

2. B. Knutson, G. W. Fong, C. M. Adams, J. L. Varner, and D. Hommer, "Dissociation of Reward Anticipation and Outcome with Event-Related FMRI." *NeuroReport* 12, no. 17 (December 4, 2001): 3683–87.

3. V. S. Ramachandran, *A Brief Tour of Human Consciousness: From Impostor Poodles to Purple Numbers* (New York: Pi Press, 2004).

4. Mathias Pessiglione, Ben Seymour, Guillaume Flandin, Raymond J. Dolan, and Chris D. Frith, "Dopamine-Dependent Prediction Errors Underpin Reward-Seeking Behaviour in Humans," *Nature* 442, no. 7106 (Aug. 2006): 1042–45, doi:10.1038/nature05051.

5. Charles B. Ferster and B. F. Skinner, *Schedules of Reinforcement* (New York: Appleton-Century-Crofts, 1957).

6. G. S. Berns, S. M. McClure, G. Pagnoni, and P. R. Montague, "Predictability Modulates Human Brain Response to Reward," *Journal of Neuroscience* 21, no. 8 (April 2001): 2793–98.

7. L. Aharon, N. Etcoff, D. Ariely, C. F. Habris, et al., "Beautiful Faces Have Variable Reward Value: fMRI and Behavioral Evidence," *Neuron* 32, no. 3 (Nov. 2001): 537–551.

8. Albert Bandura, *Social Foundations of Thought and Action: A Social Cognitive Theory* (Englewood Cliffs, NJ: Prentice Hall, 1986).

9. Albert Bandura, *Self-Efficacy: The Exercise of Self-Control* (New York: W. H. Freeman, 1997).

10. Christian Nutt, "Why Humanizing Players and Developers Is Crucial for *League of Legends*," Gamasutra (accessed Nov. 12, 2013), http://www.gamasutra.com/view/news/36847/Why_Hu manizing_Players_And_Developers_Is_Crucial_For_League _of_Legends.php.

11. Christian Nutt, "*League of Legends*: Changing Bad Player Behavior with Neuroscience," Gamasutra (accessed Nov. 12, 2013), http://www.gamasutra.com/view/news/178650/League_of _Legends_Changing_bad_player_behavior_with_neuro science.php.

12. Katharine Milton, "A Hypothesis to Explain the Role of Meat-Eating in Human Evolution," *Evolutionary Anthropology: Issues, News, and Reviews* 8, no. 1 (1999): 11–21, doi:10.1002/(SICI)1520-6505(1999)8:1<11::AID-EVAN6>3.0.CO;2-M.

13. Alok Jha, "Stone Me! Spears Show Early Human Species Was Sharper Than We Thought," *Guardian* (Nov. 15, 2012), http:// www.theguardian.com/science/2012/nov/15/stone-spear -early-human-species.

14. Robin McKie, "Humans Hunted for Meat 2 Million Years Ago," *Guardian* (Sept. 22, 2012), http://www.theguardian.com/science /2012/sep/23/human-hunting-evolution-2million-years.

15. "The Barefoot Professor: By Nature Video," video, (2010), http://www.youtube.com/watch?v=7jrnj-7YKZE.

16. Gary Rivlin, "Slot Machines for the Young and Active," *New York Times* (Dec. 10, 2007), http://www.nytimes.com/2007/12/10/business/10slots.html.

17. Amy Gesenhues, "Pinterest Says It Has 250 Million Active Monthly Users," *Marketing Land* (September 10, 2018), https://marketingland.com/pinterest-says-it-has-250-million-active-monthly-users-247779.

18. B. Zeigarnik, "Uber das Behalten yon erledigten und un-derledigten Handlungen." *Psychologische Forschung* 9 (1927): 1–85.

19. Edward L. Deci and Richard M. Ryan, "Self-determination Theory: A Macrotheory of Human Motivation, Development, and Health," *Canadian Psychology/Psychologie Canadienne* 49, no. 3 (2008): 182–85, doi:10.1037/a0012801.

20. Thomas Ricker, "Don't Fear Gmail's Priority Inbox, It Could Change Your Life," *The Verge* (July 14, 2015), https://www.theverge.com/2015/7/14/8957849/gmail-priority-inbox-changed-my-life.

21. Quantcast audience profile for mahalo.com (according to Jason Calcanis), Quantcast.com (accessed June 19, 2010), https://www.quantcast.com/mahalo.com.

22. Graham Cluley, "Creepy Quora Erodes Users' Privacy, Reveals What You Have Read," *Naked Security* (accessed Dec. 1, 2013), http://nakedsecurity.sophos.com/2012/08/09/creepy-quora-erodes-users-privacy-reveals-what-you-have-read.

23. Sandra Liu Huang, "Removing Feed Stories About Views," Quora (accessed Nov. 12, 2013), http://www.quora.com/perma link/gG922bywy.

24. Christopher J. Carpenter, "A Meta-analysis of the Effectiveness of the 'But You Are Free' Compliance-Gaining Technique," *Communication Studies* 64, no. 1 (2013): 6–17, doi:10.1080/1051 0974.2012.727941.

25. Juho Hamari, "Social Aspects Play an Important Role in Gami-fication," *Gamification Research Network* (accessed Nov. 13, 2013), http://gamification-research.org/2013/07/social-aspects.

26. Josef Adalian, "*Breaking Bad* Returns to Its Biggest Ratings Ever," *Vulture* (accessed Nov. 13, 2013), http://www.vulture.com/2013 /08/breaking-bad-returns-to-its-biggest-ratings-ever.html.

27. Mike Janela, "Breaking Bad Cooks up Record-breaking Formula for *Guinness World Records 2014* Edition," *Guinness World Records* (accessed Nov. 13, 2013), http://www.guinnessworldrecords .com/news/2013/9/breaking-bad-cooks-up-record-breaking -formula-for-guinness-world-records-2014-edition-51000.

28. Geoff F. Kaufman and Lisa K. Libby, "Changing Beliefs and Behavior through Experience-Taking," *Journal of Personality and Social Psychology* 103, no. 1 (July 2012): 1–19, doi:10.1037/a0027525.

29. C. J. Arlotta, "*CityVille* Tops *FarmVille*'s Highest Peak of Monthly Users," *SocialTimes* (accessed Nov. 13, 2013), http://socialtimes .com/cityville-tops-farmvilles-highest-peak-of-monthly-users _b33272.

30. Zynga, Inc., Form 10-K Annual Report, 2011 (San Francisco: filed Feb. 28, 2012), http://investor.zynga.com/secfiling.cfm ?filingID=1193125-12-85761&CIK=1439404.

31. Luke Karmali, *"Mists of Pandaria* Pushes *Warcraft* Subs over 10 Million," *IGN* (Oct. 4, 2012), http://www.ign.com/articles/2012 /10/04/mists-of-pandaria-pushes-warcraft-subs-over-10-million.

Chapter 5: Investment

1. "Taiwan Teen Dies After Gaming for 40 Hours," *The Australian* (accessed Nov. 13, 2013), http://www.theaustralian.com.au /news/latest-news/taiwan-teen-dies-after-gaming-for-40 -hours/story-fn3dxix6-1226428437223.

2. James Gregory Lord, *The Raising of Money: 35 Essentials Trustees Are Using to Make a Difference* (Seattle: New Futures Press, 2010).

3. Robert B. Cialdini, *Influence: The Psychology of Persuasion* (New York: HarperCollins, 2007).

4. Michael I. Norton, Daniel Mochon, and Dan Ariely, *The* "'IKEA Effect': When Labor Leads to Love" (SSRN Scholarly Paper, Rochester, NY), *Social Science Research Network* (March 4, 2011), http://papers.ssrn.com/abstract=1777100.

5. J. L. Freedman and S. C. Fraser, "Compliance Without Pressure: The Foot-in-the-Door Technique," *Journal of Personality and Social Psychology* 4, no. 2 (1966): 196–202.

6. "Jesse Schell @ DICE2010 (Part 2)," video, (2010), http://www .youtube.com/watch?v=pPfaSxU6jyY.

7. B. J. Fogg and C. Nass, "How Users Reciprocate to Computers: An Experiment That Demonstrates Behavior Change," in *Proceedings of CHI* (ACM Press, 1997), 331–32.

8. Amanda Whitbred, "At this point @Spotify's discover weekly knows me so well that if it proposed I'd say yes," Twitter,

@amandawhitbred (Aug. 18, 2016), https://twitter.com/aman
dawhitbred/status/766388337984757760.

9. Jonathan Libov, "On Bloomberg: 'You could code Twitter in a
    day. Then you'd just need to build the network and infrastruc-
    ture.' Didn't know it was so easy!," Twitter, @libovness (Nov.
    7, 2013), https://twitter.com/libovness/status/3984514649072
    59904.

10. Andrew Min, "First Impressions Matter! 2690 of Apps Down-
    loaded in 2010 Were Used Just Once," *Localytics* (accessed July 23,
    2014), http://www.localytics.com/blog/2011/first-impressions
    -matter-26-percent-of-apps-downloaded-used-just-once.

11. Peter Farago, "App Engagement: The Matrix Reloaded,"
    Flurry (accessed Nov. 13, 2013), http://blog.flurry.com/bid/90743
    /App-Engagement-The-Matrix-Reloaded.

12. Anthony Ha, "Tinder's Sean Rad Hints at a Future Beyond
    Dating, Says the App Sees 350M Swipes a Day," *TechCrunch*
    (accessed Nov. 13, 2013), http://techcrunch.com/2013/10/29
    /sean-rad-disrupt.

13. Stuart Dredge, "Snapchat: Self-destructing Messaging App
    Raises $60M in Funding," *Guardian* (June 25, 2013), http://
    www.theguardian.com/technology/appsblog/2013/jun/25
    /snapchat-app-self-destructing-messaging.

14. Kara Swisher and Liz Gannes, "Pinterest Does Another Massive
    Funding—$225 Million at $3.8 Billion Valuation (Confirmed),"
    All Things Digital (accessed Nov. 13, 2013), http://allthingsd
    .com/20131023/pinterest-does-another-massive-funding-225
    -million-at-3-8-billion-valuation.

Chapter 6: What Are You Going to Do with This?

1. For further thoughts on the morality of designing behavior, see: Richard H. Thaler, Cass R. Sunstein, and John P. Balz, "Choice Architecture" (SSRN Scholarly Paper, Rochester, New York), *Social Science Research Network*, (April 2, 2010), http://papers.ssrn.com/abstract=1583509.

2. Charlie White, "Survey: Cellphones vs. Sex—Which Wins?," *Mashable*, http://mashable.com/2011/08/03/telenav-cellphone-infographic.

3. Ian Bogost, "The Cigarette of This Century," *Atlantic* (June 6, 2012), http://www.theatlantic.com/technology/archive/2012/06/the-cigarette-of-this-century/258092.

4. David H. Freedman, "The Perfected Self," *Atlantic* (June 2012), http://www.theatlantic.com/magazine/archive/2012/06/the-perfected-self/308970.

5. Paul Graham,"The Acceleration of Addictiveness," *Paul Graham* (July 2010; accessed Nov. 12, 2013), http://www.paulgraham.com/addiction.html.

6. Gary Bunker, "The Ethical Line in User Experience Research," *mUmBRELLA* (accessed Nov. 13, 2013), http://mumbrella.com.au/the-ethical-line-in-user-experience-research-163114.

7. Chris Nodder, "How Deceptive Is Your Persuasive Design?" *UX Magazine* (accessed Nov. 13, 2013), https://uxmag.com/articles/how-deceptive-is-your-persuasive-design.

8. "Nurturing Self-help Among Kenyan Farmers," *GSB in Brief* (accessed Dec. 1, 2013), http://www.gsb.stanford.edu/news/bmag/sbsm0911/ss-kenyan.html.

9. David Stewart, *Demystifying Slot Machines and Their Impact in the United States*, American Gaming Association (May 26, 2010), http://www.americangaming.org/sites/default/files/uploads /docs/whitepapers/demystifying_slot_machines_and_their _impact.pdf.

10. Michael Shermer, "How We Opt Out of Overoptimism: Our Habit of Ignoring What Is Real Is a Double-Edged Sword," *Scientific American* (accessed Nov. 13, 2013), http://www.scientific american.com/article.cfm?id=opting-out-of-overoptimism.

11. Jason Tanz, "The Curse of Cow Clicker: How a Cheeky Satire Became a Videogame Hit," *Wired* (accessed Nov. 13, 2013), http://www.wired.com/magazine/2011/12/ff_cowclicker.

12. Ian Bogost, "Cowpocalypse Now: The Cows Have Been Raptured," Bogost.com (accessed Nov. 13, 2013), http://www.bogost .com/blog/cowpocalypse_now.shtml

Chapter 7: Case Studies

1. "On Fifth Anniversary of Apple iTunes Store, YouVersion Bible App Reaches 100 Million Downloads: First-Ever Survey Shows How App Is Truly Changing Bible Engagement," *PRWeb* (July 8, 2013), http://www.prweb.com/releases/2013/7/prweb109055 95.htm.

2. Alexia Tsotsis,"Snapchat Snaps Up a $80M Series B Led by IVP at an $800M Valuation," *TechCrunch* (accessed Nov. 13, 2013), http://techcrunch.com/2013/06/22/source-snapchat-snaps -up-80m-from-ivp-at-a-800m-valuation.

3. YouVersion infographics (accessed Nov. 13, 2013), http://blog .youversion.com/wp-content/uploads/2013/07/themobile bible1.jpg.

4. Henry Alford, "If I Do Humblebrag So Myself," *New York Times* (Nov. 30, 2012), http://www.nytimes.com/2012/12/02/fashion/bah-humblebrag-the-unfortunate-rise-of-false-humility.html.

5. Diana I. Tamir and Jason P. Mitchell, "Disclosing Information About the Self Is Intrinsically Rewarding," *Proceedings of the National Academy of Sciences* (May 7, 2012): 201202129, doi:10.1073/pnas.1202129109.

6. Sarah O'Brien, "Americans Spend $56 Billion on Sporting Events," September 11, 2017, https://www.cnbc.com/2017/09/11/americans-spend-56-billion-on-sporting-events.html.

7. "Attendance, Adherence, Drop out and Retention," PT-Direct (accessed November 28, 2018), https://www.ptdirect.com/training-design/exercise-behaviour-and-adherence/attendance-adherence-drop-out-and-retention-patterns-of-gym-members.

8. "Future Self: Hyperbolic Discounting (a Cognitive Bias) in Life Choices," Nir and Far, August 9, 2017, https://www.nirandfar.com/2017/08/hyperbolic-discounting-why-you-make-terrible-life-choices.html

9. "Fitbod for iOS: Personalized Strength Training powered by machine learning," *Medium* (accessed December 13, 2018), https://medium.com/fitbod-blog/fitbod-for-ios-press-kit-fae708e925bd.

Chapter 8: Habit Testing and Where to Look for Habit-Forming Opportunities

1. Mattan Griffel, "Discovering Your Aha! Moment," *GrowHack* (Dec. 4, 2012), http://www.growhack.com/2012/12/04/discovering-your-aha-moment.

2. Paul Graham, "Schlep Blindness," *Paul Graham* (Jan. 2012), http://paulgraham.com/schlep.html.

3. Joel Gascoigne, "Buffer October Update: $2,388,000 Annual Revenue Run Rate, 1,123,000 Users," Buffer (Nov. 7, 2013), http://open.bufferapp.com/buffer-october-update-2388000 -run-rate-1123000-users.

4. Tessa Miller, "I'm Joel Gascoigne, and This Is the Story Behind Buffer," *Life Hacker* (accessed Nov. 13, 2013), http://www.life hacker.co.in/technology/Im-Joel-Gascoigne-and-This-Is-the -Story-Behind-Buffer.

5. Nancy Martha West, *Kodak and the Lens of Nostalgia* (Charlottesville: The University Press of Virginia, 2000).

6. G. Cosier and P. M. Hughes, "The Problem with Disruption," *BT Technology* 19, no. 4 (Oct. 2001): 9.

7. Clifford A. Pickover, *Time: A Traveler's Guide* (New York: Oxford University Press, 1998).

8. Clifford Stoll, "The Internet? Bah!" *Newsweek* (Feb. 27, 1995), http://www.english.illinois.edu/-people-/faculty/debaron /582/582%20readings/stoll.pdf.

9. Mike Maples Jr., "Technology Waves and the Hypernet," *Roger and Mike's Hypernet Blog* (accessed Nov. 13, 2013), http://roger andmike.com/post/14629058018/technology-waves-and-the -hypernet.

10. Paul Graham, "How to Get Startup Ideas." *Paul Graham* (Nov. 2012), http://paulgraham.com/startupideas.html.